MW01599817

SHAKTI

SHAKTI

Stories of Indian Women in South Africa

Compiled by Alleyn Diesel

Wits University Press
1 Jan Smuts Avenue
Johannesburg
2001
http://witspress.wits.ac.za

Copyright © Alleyn Diesel, 2007

First published 2007

ISBN 978-1-86814-454-9

All rights reserved. No part of this publication may be reproduced, stored in a retrieval system, or transmitted in any form or by any means, electronic, mechanical, photocopying, recording or otherwise, without the prior permission of the copyright holder.

Design and layout by Hybridesign
Photographs by Alleyn Diesel except on page x,
    courtesy of the Local History Museum Collection, Durban
Printed and bound by Creda Communications

Contents

Preface

Since 1987 I have been speaking to Hindu women about their interest and participation in religious activities, particularly the worship of the various goddesses of the Hindu tradition. In various articles I have written of my admiration for the independence and determination shown by numerous women, and my conviction that their devotion to the fierce, autonomous goddesses such as Kali, Mariamman and Draupadi has provided them with empowering role models, allowing them to act with confidence and to attain a reasonably high profile and some recognition in their communities. A number of these women, such as Pat Pillay in this collection, are involved in religious healing which has brought them considerable respect and status (Diesel 1998 a & b; 2002).

The more Indian women I have talked to, the more I have come to realise that almost all of them have interesting, sometimes compelling, stories to tell that demonstrate their strength and determination in adversity, and their pride in their ancient culture and religion. They are also remarkably articulate in the telling of these stories. However, it seems clear to me that in recent years the collecting of the stories of people in the so-called 'previously disadvantaged' communities in South Africa has so far almost completely overlooked the experiences of Indian women – Hindu, Muslim and Christian, which constitutes the loss of a vibrant and vital section of this country's colourful and varied population.

I am aware that some feminists believe that 'privileged' White women should not write or 'speak for' women whose voices have generally been silenced by their circumstances of oppression. But when I have expressed such reservations to the women I have spoken to, they have assured me of their willingness, even enthusiasm, for me to record their stories and present them to a wider audience. I do not wish to speak 'on behalf of' anyone, but merely to provide a platform for the women's voices to be heard. I believe that, in post-apartheid South Africa, this stringently 'politically correct' categorising of who may or may not write about whom should no longer continue since the Constitution now protects all individuals and groups from discrimination on the grounds of colour, creed, gender, and sexual orientation. Wherever possible, I have allowed the women to speak for themselves, in their own words as captured on a tape recorder. Each woman in this collection has seen what has been written about her and has expressed her satisfaction with the tone and accuracy of her story.

These stories would not otherwise have been recorded. I believe they are valuable for a number of reasons, not merely for the entertainment they provide. First, they contain fascinating aspects of local history, such as life in the largely Hindi-speaking community in Edendale/Plessislaer before the forced removals, and the founding of the Indian Women's Association; as well as a glimpse into Indian women's religious, social and political activities that have not always been given due attention in the wider Pietermaritzburg community. Second, they reveal the women's view of themselves in a society that has often been unwelcoming, even hostile: their sense of their own worth and their contribution, however small, to the building of a better social order; and their confidence that, as women, they can claim their rightful place in a country that – hopefully – is becoming increasingly aware of the value of each individual, regardless of racial, sexual, cultural or religious identity. Third, in South Africa at present there is a great challenge to learn to appreciate and celebrate rather than to fear and harbour suspicions about the religious and cultural beliefs and practices of others. Tolerance comes from understanding more about other people's traditions, which can be facilitated by respectfully listening to one another's stories.

I hope that many women from a variety of backgrounds will appreciate and enjoy these stories. I believe they will be able to identify with the joys and achievements, but also sympathise with the difficulties and sadnesses recorded. At various points many women are likely to think, 'Yes, that's just like my life; I understand that.' And some men, too, may be moved to admire the determination and courage displayed in these accounts.

The word *Shakti* means the power or energy of women. *Shakti* is often believed to be personified and expressed by divine females, those alter egos of every woman, who are amply portrayed in these accounts of the experiences of local Indian women.

Acknowledgements

I wish to thank Jerry Frazer, former librarian at *The Witness*, for all her help in tracing previously published material; Nalini Naidoo, also of *The Witness*, for advice and encouragement; Jewel Koopman and Estelle Liebenberg of the Alan Paton Centre at the University of KwaZulu-Natal (UKZN) for their help and encouragement; Julia Braine of the UKZN Student Counselling and Careers Centre for supplying statistics about Indian women's career choices; Kobus Moolman for reading and commenting on some of the stories; Pat Pillay for teaching me so much about her devotion to the fierce goddess Kali; and my partner Mary Kleinenberg for her patient and ongoing encouragement throughout the process of compiling these stories. In addition, much appreciation goes to Wits University Press for showing their confidence in the worth of the manuscript by agreeing to publish it. Finally, and most importantly, a huge 'thank you' to all the women participants who so eagerly agreed to be part of the project, many of whom warmly welcomed me into their homes.

ix

Introduction
Women in the South African Indian community

Indians began to arrive in the British colony of Natal in November 1860 as indentured labourers hired to work on the coastal sugar estates north and south of the port of Durban. About ten years later, various other groups of immigrants started arriving in the colony and became known as 'passenger' Indians since they had paid for their own passages and held British travel documents. Most indentured labourers were Tamils from around the south Indian city of Madras (now Chennai), belonging largely to the Sudra (labourer) class. More indentured workers from the northern areas of Bihar and Uttar Pradesh arrived later. The 'passenger' Indians, many of whom came from around Bombay and Gujarat, were economically better off. Their reason for coming to Natal was mainly as traders, bringing much needed and prized Indian goods to the outlying communities of homesick immigrants. Most of these people were Muslims, while the vast majority of the indentured people – approximately ninety per cent – were Hindu (Pillay et al. 1989:146). The 'passenger' population has been estimated as approximately ten per cent of those who arrived in the early years of immigration (Lemon 1990:131). Altogether, just over 150 000 indentured Indians were brought to Natal in the fifty-year period between 1860 and 1911, after which the Indian government put a stop to the system of indenture, largely in response to a public outcry in India about conditions encountered by fellow compatriots in South Africa.

The Hindus who came to Natal belonged to four language groups. The approximate size of these groups in the South African Hindu population at present is as follows: Tamils: 45 per cent; Telugus: 18 per cent; Hindi speakers: 30 per cent; and Gujaratis: 7 per cent. However, recent census figures indicate that 95 per cent of Indian South Africans now speak English as their first language (Freund 1995:9, 87).

The traditional caste/class system has never been much observed in South Africa, largely because people from a variety of backgrounds, social classes, geographical areas and religions were forced to mix. Since the majority of the Hindu labourers were from the lower castes, they stood to gain nothing by attempting to maintain a system that discriminated against them. However, people maintained their Indian identity through their language and religious practices.

The early immigrants found life in their new country extremely difficult. Family life was so drastically disrupted that it became almost non-existent. Poor housing and wages, long working hours, malnourishment and unhygienic conditions were the norm, with a high mortality rate. The immigrants frequently complained about their living and working conditions, and many desperate people committed suicide.

 2

Although the Indian government required that four women be brought to South Africa for every ten men, few women were initially prepared to undertake the difficult and daunting journey from their homeland to face new and uncertain conditions. Eventually, however, numbers of Indian women – many of whom were young widows, or deserted by husbands, or disowned by families, and often poor and sickly – were driven by desperation to offer themselves for indentures. In Natal their existence was often no better than in India, where they found themselves unwelcome, often hugely overworked, and with employers only interested in strong, healthy men. Furthermore, a great deal of confusion surrounded the conditions of women's employment. Many women were dreadfully exploited, both by employers and by their fellow male compatriots, with numerous accounts of women being bought, sold and given away in return for rations, clothing, or other (often sexual) favours. Indentured women, when they were paid at all, were the lowest-paid workers in the colony, right at the bottom of the class-race-gender hierarchy (Beall 1990:150–151, 155–156, 159, 166).

After completing their ten-year contracts, many labourers chose to remain in Natal, moving to the city of Durban and the surrounding areas where they became engaged in market gardening, hawking, fishing, and domestic work, as well as in the Durban and Pietermaritzburg municipalities. Others found employment in the Northern Natal coal mines and in the Natal government railways. Many continued growing sugar cane, acquiring their own smallholdings. Market gardeners were engaged in the production of fruit and vegetables, largely for White consumption. Some managed to establish small shops from which to sell their produce. The women of these families usually became actively involved in both the growing and marketing of the produce, working extremely hard at heavy manual labour. Women hawkers with heavy baskets of vegetables and fruit on their heads became a familiar sight in the White suburbs of Durban and Pietermaritzburg.

3

This move to towns and cities began the urbanisation process of the South African Indian population. By 1985, approximately 91 per cent of Indians in Natal lived in urban areas (Freund 1995:13). However, most Indians remained extremely poor, having to work very hard for small returns and with few opportunities for improvement.

According to Beall (1990), the only options for women after the expiry of their indentures were 'repatriation, marriage, or some other form of dependence on a male partner or relative'. There is evidence that the practice of child marriage, highly condemned by neo-Hindu (reform) groups in India and outlawed there in 1929, was regularly practised in Natal, with accounts of girls as young as ten and twelve years old having marriages arranged for them.

As Indians moved out of the indenture system, the extended family system began to be reconstructed, which established a much-needed security for its members. It is important to bear in mind, however, that the patriarchal family structure also resulted in oppressive relationships and considerable violence against women.

Indians began to arrive and settle in Pietermaritzburg from about 1863. They were mainly Hindi- and Tamil-speaking Hindus. They acquired properties in the lower Church and Longmarket Street area where they soon established houses, market gardens, stores and temples. The Knipe Street barracks were built to house municipal labourers. Indian families also later spread into Raisethorpe. This whole area became recognised as having a distinctive Indian flavour and, by 1898, it has been estimated that there were approximately three thousand Indians living in the city. In the 1880s Muslim merchants, often referred to as 'Arabs' to distinguish them from the previously indentured Hindu people, began to open shops in the upper Church Street area where they soon attracted considerable Black trade (Wills 1988:37f).

Later, groups of Indians moved out of the central city grid of Pietermaritzburg to establish market gardens and smallholdings along the Dorpspruit near Camps Drift, and further south in the Mason's Mill, Plessislaer and Foxhill areas.

 4 During 1914, the Gandhi-led *Satyagraha* (non-violence/passive resistance) campaign – started in 1906 to agitate for justice in the face of laws that discriminated against South African Indians – attracted large numbers of immensely enthusiastic women, who marched great distances across northern Natal into the Transvaal. These women were willing to be arrested, to endure extremely difficult conditions, and to make public speeches in support of the action.

Again, during the Passive Resistance Campaign in 1946, a number of women in Durban were among the protesters against the 'Ghetto Act'. They pitched tents and camped on vacant municipal land on the corner of Gale Street and Umbilo Road, continuing to defy the law over the many months that followed, despite being arrested and charged on numerous occasions.

In the 1950s and 1960s, the apartheid 'Group Areas' legislation brought severe and tragic disruptions. Whole communities, by now fairly settled and integrated, were ruthlessly uprooted from their homes, businesses, schools and religious institutions, and forced into inferior housing with no choice of area or neighbours, and usually with utterly inadequate compensation. It has been estimated that up to 80 per cent of the Durban Indian population was moved under the forced removals programme (Freund 1995:64).

Thousands of people from the central areas of the city were taken to the new working class community of Chatsworth, opened in 1964, and situated far from the city and people's places of work and traditional places of worship. Freund has described it as 'a separate Indian city detached from Durban and its resources' (1995:89). Other working class Durban Indians were resettled in Newlands and Phoenix to the north. Two, more affluent, areas were created at Isipingo Beach to the south and at Reservoir Hills, near the newly created Indian University of Durban-Westville. In Pietermaritzburg, Indians were also moved from the secure, lush, mixed-race settlements in the Edendale, Plessislaer, Pentrich and Foxhill areas, where a largely Hindi-speaking community had lived since before the turn of the nineteenth century, to the new suburb of Northdale on the other side of the city, in which they were accommodated in small, poorly-built houses. Although some families expressed satisfaction about the new, more modern accommodation, many extended families were forced to split up because of the small houses. This caused considerable hardship, particularly for the aged, as well as greater expense, above all in rent and transport. In many cases relocation broke social contacts within what had been well-established, supportive communities. Resources in the new areas were initially dismally poor, with shops, schools and health facilities often only being provided considerably later. New places of worship also had to be constructed at great expense.

These upsets, especially the break-up of the extended family, have had profoundly negative effects on many in the Indian community, resulting in feelings of frustration, depression, discontent, and a general sense of loss of dignity. Nevertheless, with characteristic tenacity, these large groups of displaced people have battled to reorganise themselves, rebuilding their lives in the new areas. However, alcoholism, crime, violence against women, and divorce rates have become increasingly prevalent, indications of the stress associated with a lack of recognition as a community and with social change.

A further negative consequence of apartheid policies has been the harm done to race relations, resulting in 'Indians of all classes [feeling] a sense of antagonism and distance from whites' (Freund 1995:84). The damage to Indian/

5

African relations is also an ongoing problem. Fortunately, by 1980 the process of removals began to slow down and the 'grand plan' was never fully implemented.

In the workplace, from 1960 onwards, rapid industrial expansion – particularly centred round Durban – provided much needed work for many Indians. Many were employed as semi-skilled workers in the textile and clothing industry and, from 1970, the number of skilled workers increased markedly. An additional significant development in the 1960s was the number of Indian women who moved away from traditional domestic duties to start work in the factories. Over the years this trend has increased. As women have become better educated, they have moved into office work, business, and the professions.

Since the 1990s, increasing numbers of Indian women have attended the University of Natal (now UKZN) in both Durban and Pietermaritzburg. There they have received professional training, particularly in law, commerce, the social sciences and medicine, to the extent that their presence and contribution are now highly visible in these cities.

 6

Unfortunately, becoming wage earners has not necessarily given women independence from patriarchal control. Traditional Indian families have tended to regard women as having a subordinate status to men, with the expectation that their primary roles are those of wife and mother. This has resulted in many women being largely confined to the home, engaged almost entirely in domestic activities. Generally women are discouraged from gaining a separate, independent identity. Their identity is acquired from a male relative: father, husband, or eldest son after the husband's death. Religion – Hinduism, Islam, and Christianity – has largely worked to maintain this attitude, often portraying women as not only physically weaker than men but also intellectually and morally inferior, to perpetuate their subordination. Thus, women are generally not acknowledged as full members of their religious community, their contribution being regarded as secondary and simply supportive. As a result, men's voices, decisions and achievements dominate. Women's voices are not usually considered valuable enough to be heard, so their activities and interests remain unrecognised on the whole.

Most religious traditions have now begun to accommodate changes to improve the lot of women. Too often, however, these tend to be offered in a patronising, half-hearted manner. Women are assured that indeed they have 'an equal but different' role, which merely perpetuates their subservience.

In spite of this male dominance, Indian women have demonstrated their strength and determination in many ways, regularly breaking out of their domestic confines to attend educational institutions, as indicated above. Often they have achieved a remarkable independence and influence, even within the limitations of their domestic lives. Indian women continue to demonstrate their interest in and commitment to religious matters, frequently forming the majority of devotees at religious gatherings and sometimes performing fairly high-profile tasks, often finding considerable satisfaction in daily home-based and life-cycle rituals such as the preparation of food for various occasions and the conveying of religious traditions to children. All these activities give structure and meaning to their lives. But they do not constitute any real challenge to the overall patriarchal control of religion or to the establishment of a more egalitarian social order in which women's voices are accorded full recognition.

Apartheid legislation denied people their heritage and its accompanying sense of identity. Therefore, like many other groups, Indians who suffered from oppression need to reclaim their memories and proudly acknowledge their Indian origins and culture. As a diaspora community, they are constantly faced with multiple identities: Indian, south/north Indian, Hindu/Muslim/Christian, South African, Eastern/Asian, and Western. For women, this is further complicated by the fact that their 'triple oppression' under apartheid discrimination in terms of being 'non-White', female, and often poor, has made the question of 'Who am I?' a challenging one, not easily answered. But there is increasing evidence that Indian women's proven tenacity in adversity as well as their firm sense of their own worth will allow them to continue to make a valuable contribution in an environment which, hopefully, will facilitate greater opportunity and well-being for them than has been offered in the past.

7

Grandmother's feet

Raaz Pillay

Raaz Pillay also calls herself Doris. But her given name is Raazamah from the word Rajamah, meaning kingly or royalty, reflecting the high hopes of her parents. Born in Estcourt in 1935, Raaz attended the Pietermaritzburg Indian Girls' High School up to Standard 8, but later completed her matric and qualified as a teacher with an M3 diploma at Springfield Training College. She now lives in Pietermaritzburg where she represents the African Christian Democratic Party in local government politics. This story is part of a longer piece consisting of a number of stories about her family which, after a writing workshop – 'We are the stories we tell' – organised in 1998 by Dr K Kendall of the University of KwaZulu-Natal Drama Department, was housed in the Alan Paton Centre on the campus. This is an important piece because of its historical interest in supplying various first-hand details of the experiences of first-generation indentured immigrants from India. (The name 'Ouwa' used here for her grandmother is the Telugu equivalent of the Tamil 'Aiya'.)

Ouwa, my grandmother, reached for a large bottle that stood on a low shelf attached to the wall. The bottle was filled with a soft white greasy paste. She had carefully made this paste with two-thirds melted candle wax and one-third paraffin. The paste was applied to her arms and feet as a moisturiser, every evening during the winter months. First, she washed her feet in warm water using soap and a piece of coir to remove the grime. Ouwa loved walking around barefoot. Although she took great care, her fingers and feet were rough and red and seemed to have been neglected when she was younger. Her small toe on each foot stood at right angles to her other toes. I thought she had deliberately allowed them to grow that way because of some ritual or other reason. She wore white canvas sand shoes. Exactly in the area of her smallest toes, she had cut out two holes to allow her toes to stick out or else her shoes would not fit. It looked odd. I was amused. I was tempted to ask her occasionally about her toes, but I did not have the courage to do so. Sometimes I wanted to laugh, but no-one was allowed to make fun of Ouwa. She was respected as a senior member of the family.

 10

We were sitting around the *bowla* on the verandah. It was a fire of wood or coal made in a large, empty paraffin tin punched full of holes. The holes allowed the heat to escape. Because there was no electricity, we had to improvise in order to ward off the cold. The dry wood crackled sharply, sending off bright sparks as we basked in the warmth that emanated from it. When the fire in the kitchen stove burned itself out after the preparation of the evening meal, the family gathered round the *bowla*. It was unhealthy and dangerous to keep the *bowla* inside where it would create a lot of smoke and cause damage, so Ouwa decided that the verandah was the best place for it.

'Why is your small toe facing the other way, Ouwa?' I suddenly asked her that evening.

Ouwa often referred to the female members of the family as 'Ma'. 'Ma,' said Ouwa, 'me, Thatha (my grandfather) working koilarbarns.'

'What is koilarbarns, Ouwa?'

'You see, Ma, me show you, heh.' She hastily went into the yard and brought back a small rusty old bucket with coal in it. She pointed to the coal and said, 'See, koilar – by the Newcastle; beeg hole. Ma, wait I'm tell you nice, you hearing nice.' Finding it awkward to continue in English, she explained in Telugu, her mother tongue. Ouwa, Thatha, Ama (my mother), and all my brothers and sisters communicated in Telugu.

Ouwa explained that the ship in which they travelled from India to Durban belonged to the British. Natal was part of the British Colony. You see, Ouwa was born to high-caste parents. Their trade was jewellery-making, which elevated them to a high status. She was accustomed to a comfortable life. When she got married she was just thirteen years old. She could not understand or get on with her mother-in-law, so she left India because she was so severely ill-treated by her. Being young and desperate, she saw an opportunity when a ship was ready to leave India for Durban, so she quickly seized her infant son and secretly fled from her family, only to be caught up in oppression of a different kind in the coal mines in Newcastle.

When Ouwa boarded the ship she came as a single person with a year-old son. Ouwa and Thatha befriended each other on the ship and were paired off by the authorities when they reached Durban. They were regarded as man and wife, and taken to Newcastle by a White man. They had no choice. Their future lay in the hands of the man who collected them when they disembarked. They arrived in Newcastle, were given a place to stay, and made to work in the coal mines (koilarbarns).

They woke at four every morning and proceeded to work. Many Indian families were employed there already. Their homes were close to each other. Ouwa wore no shoes then. She could not afford them. When she had hurriedly and secretly left India, she had left behind most of her possessions. During winter it was extremely cold. Frost was a daily occurrence and intermittent falls of snow plunged the countryside into freezing conditions.

This was when it happened, she said. Huge blocks of coal fell out of a very large wagon. One block fell on her feet and knocked her right over. It was very painful for her to recall the facts, as she told us. She spoke with a heavy heart and wiped away tears with the edge of her sari. The damage was severe, she said. Some of her toes were broken, her ankle was broken, and her feet were swollen for many months afterwards. She did not get help from a professional doctor, but used home remedies.

I now understood the unusual position of her toes. She showed us her damaged heels. There were large cracks but the wounds had healed, leaving wide gaping spaces. It reminded me of soil erosion. The cuts were not as wide as they were deep. Sometimes they would bleed and cause pain and discomfort. These cuts were also the result of walking barefoot in freezing conditions. Ouwa told us that this was the most difficult time of her life. More tears as she sobbed bitterly. It had made her wonder whether coming away from India was a good idea after all.

'Raazamah,' she said, 'Thatha, I working too hard, Ma. Lil'bit money; twaalif shillin, Ma, pick work.'

'But, Ouwa,' I said, 'you are so brave. Why didn't you go away to another place, just how you came away from India?'

'Nor, Ma, nor, nor; we work for girrimit (government), carn' go; can die.' She was referring to the five-year term that each indentured labourer had to serve before he or she could be released. At the end of this period, the labourer could stay on or be released. Ouwa and Thatha worked there for fifteen years. In their position they could not change from one employer to another, they could not ask for more money or rations of food. They had no choice. Their future remained bleak, except that every third year a new member was added to their family, so life got tougher.

 12

'Why did you have so many children, Ouwa, because it is not so easy to care for them?'

'God gave, Ma; what to do?' Ouwa was serious about this. 'Some peoples carn' get no childrens. You got house, you can got lot childrens too.'

We were puzzled, but said nothing.

They made maximum use of the gardens allotted to them. At harvest time Ouwa packed the produce into baskets. She pointed to a basket that had held vegetables. This basket was of sentimental value to her; she had kept it for many years, fastened to a hook near the ceiling. This strong woven basket had two compartments to hold produce. When they had time to spare they marketed their produce. Gardens around their homes were great opportunities for resourceful people to supplement their incomes.

Ouwa told us about the foreman, the *sirdar*, an Indian who took great care of the whole settlement. There had to be no trouble in the mines or in the domestic lives of the people. A sjambok was the weapon used to threaten defaulters. He was a stern man. He wore a huge turban on his head, which made him look and feel important. Heavy gold earrings pulled his earlobes down and caused them to sag. On hot days he wore a *dhoti* that went round his waist and between his legs. He meted out punishment ruthlessly if someone caused a problem. Lashes from a whip, the payment of a fine, or isolation from the family was the price to be paid.

Distance from India created a sadness hard to survive in this strange place, and they had to adopt a positive attitude. The community tried to recapture the life they had known back in India. They tried to normalise the situation. Gathering together in the evenings and weekends was a common practice in which music and singing regularly featured. Various activities were organised and people displayed their artistic talents through dramatisation and storytelling. Religious practice continued, and cultural customs were fiercely promoted. The pivotal role played by feasts and festivals contributed to the warmth and growth of a vibrant community. To preserve the quality of their rich heritage, spicy foods and traditional dress were adhered to as much as possible.

13 ❀

•

Veersamy Naidoo, Ouwa's son who came with her from India, was the eldest child, followed by two daughters Nagamah and Yenkamah, then two more sons. Veersamy, now a teenager, was employed by the railways. Thatha terminated his services at the mines when his third contract expired. He also got a job on the railways and the whole family moved to Estcourt, which made it easier to travel to and from work.

In Estcourt, Zaaylager Farm was the place where Indians lived. A few businessmen were sparsely scattered in the city centre. The farm was well populated, but there were no educational, health or business facilities. The Indians developed Zaaylager into a thriving settlement. Yenkamah, now an attractive twelve year old with two long, flowing plaits, wore a skirt that reached her ankles. She was keen to improve the quality of her life. Both she and her sister, Nagamah, observed neighbours and friends using a sewing machine. This triggered a thirst for knowledge and the intricacies involved in operating one of these machines were quickly learned. Their enthusiasm knew no bounds. They began cutting out garments freehand. They made simple articles of clothing for themselves.

Crocheting also captured their interest. Once again, their keen observation acquired for them the delicate skills involved. Crocheting yards of fine lace to attach to their underskirts was their speciality, as well as making attractive sets of doilies to adorn the table. Producing a dainty 'shimmie' (chemise) brought compliments from family members and friends. Their creative efforts went further as knitting became another pastime. The composition of a pattern was discovered by unravelling an old garment row by row, studying the arrangement of stitches of the previous row, and then reconstructing the pattern anew.

Yenkamah collected newspapers from neighbours. On spring-cleaning day she would sit down and fold the paper diagonally four times, then she carefully cut around one edge with a pair of scissors. She snipped here and trimmed there until she was satisfied. She opened out the paper and held it up. Beautiful patterns emerged. These decorative sheets were placed on shelves that held beautiful, gleaming brass ornaments. She enjoyed her hobbies very much and moved from simple things to more complicated ones. But her life was soon to change.

·

Chinniah left India as a seventeen year old. He was tempted by the attractive promises made by the British. He had practically no knowledge of Natal. Many single men had already left his home town and he planned to leave too. Chinniah's parents were not aware of what he was contemplating. One day he quickly left home. He spent three days concealed in a very tall tree. He clambered down at night and stole round secretly, enquiring from his friends whether his parents had discovered his plans and when the ship was due to sail. When he was hungry, he ate coconuts. On the third night he was told that the ship was leaving the next day. He cautiously joined the queue, sneaked past the officials, and smuggled himself on board. Then he hid. Crouching low among the bags in the storage room, he avoided people. He came out sometimes when it was safe and mingled with others, undetected. After two days out at sea, he went out on deck during the early evening and, when he returned to his hideout, the door had been securely locked. He waited a long while in the shadows, then grew tired and fell asleep. Someone tugged at his shirt, and shouted. The man had been sweeping the deck and discovered the stowaway. The captain was summoned and it was discovered that this young man was not on the ship's register and did not have any personal documents. So he was given a number and made to assist the workers, and allowed to continue to Natal.

He befriended a couple and remained with them when they disembarked in Durban. A White man took them to Richmond, where they worked on his farm. People were distributed throughout the length and breadth of Natal, some to the coal mines, some to sugar plantations, others to private farms. On this ship there were also traders and merchants who set up their own businesses.

When his first contract was over, Chinniah moved to Greytown. Being young and single, he was free to do as he wished. He found employment and married a young girl and settled down. Not long after that, tragedy struck. His young wife died and he was alone again. He got involved in the building trade by assisting building contractors. Soon he became an experienced builder and set up as an independent contractor. His work took him to many places throughout Natal. He was working comfortably on a new contract in Estcourt when something happened that changed his life.

Nagamah had married Murugas Govender and assisted him in their dry-cleaning business in Estcourt. Yenkamah, her sister, often brought them delicacies from home. She was proud of her culinary skills. One day she rushed in nervously, raising her voice, very upset indeed. Tears welled up in her eyes and spilled over. Her sister was concerned: 'What's wrong Yenkamah, come quick and tell me.' Yenkamah pointed to a newly constructed building. 'That man, that stupid man is calling me. Every time I pass he calls me. Today he followed me. I'm so frightened. He is up to something.' Nagamah consoled her and advised her not to worry, but to walk on the other side of the road.

Yenkamah took her sister's advice and, on her return, walked briskly. She almost ran past the high wall next to the newly constructed building. She turned her face away, thinking that she could escape unnoticed. This was not to be. Bump! came a sound a few feet in front of her. It was an apple, which rolled towards

15 ❁

her. She looked up, guessing where it came from. 'Ayeore!' she exclaimed, picking up the apple. The rude man was amused. He laughed in a carefree manner and walked to the edge of the roof. Then he shouted out, '*Ponare, ponare*', meaning 'Girl, girl'. Trembling with rage, Yenkamah flung the apple away, picked up her long skirt and raced off, hoping never to set eyes on him ever again. But a serious drama was unfolding.

By evening she was calm and was trying to forget the day's events. Occupied with her evening chores, she hummed a tune. She thought she heard a knocking on the door. It was unusual for visitors to come knocking at this hour. Her curiosity aroused, Yenkamah reluctantly opened the door. This was unbelievable. There on the doorstep, hat in hand, stood the crazy man from the roof top. Her reaction was understandable. She turned round and disappeared into the kitchen, her heart pounding as if it would burst. Ouwa, realising that something was the matter, went to the door that was still ajar. A strange man stood there asking if he could come in for a short while. Ouwa and Thatha exchanged greetings with him. He had to state his name and the reason for his visit. He said he had come to complain about the young girl who had been rude to him. Ouwa was disappointed with Yenkamah's behaviour as she had often told her that male members of the community had to be respected. Yenkamah was reprimanded and made to apologise. She was highly embarrassed, and annoyed too, as she could do or say nothing to defend herself.

This was the beginning of a close friendship between her parents and the stranger. The visits became more frequent. They all had a common topic of conversation: India, and the families they had left behind. Yenkamah was always out of view, but within earshot. She realised that this man was not a monster she must avoid but a lonely man with few friends and no immediate family. To Yenkamah's surprise, one day Ouwa announced that the strange builder who visited them regularly had asked for her hand in marriage. His name was Chinniah, and they had all been on the ship together. Ouwa said that, after consideration, she and Thatha had consented. Yenkamah was not consulted and she knew her complaints would fall on deaf ears. It was ridiculous to complain, so she slowly grew accustomed to the idea and, in time, found herself making preparations for the wedding.

 16

The celebrations started a couple of weeks before the wedding. Two weeks previously an elderly man clad in a *dhoti* and turban walked from door to door announcing the wedding. This was an official invitation to the ceremony and to partake in the feast afterwards. On a beautiful spring evening thirty-eight-year-old Chinniah Pillay married attractive thirteen-year-old Yenkamah Narsirmulu. Being the youngest daughter, there was cause for great jubilation. The *pundal* (tent) where the wedding was held was brightly decorated with marigolds and banana leaves. On the ground were filigreed patterns about two metres square, which were made by squeezing mealie meal between the forefinger and thumb and letting it drop gently to form designs as the hand moved. Garlands of marigolds hung on heavy brass pots and decorated doorways. A long wooden stool stood on a grass mat in the *pundal*, which the bridal couple sat on. A tall brass candlestick burned brightly. The local Brahmin officiated. Lilting music filled the air and songs were sung to the accompaniment of musical instruments. The sacred symbol of marriage, the *thali,* was in the form of a gold coin, with a yellow string attached to it. It was reverently placed round the bride's neck and knotted several times by the bridegroom. Rings were placed on both her longest toes.

17

The couple settled down in their own home a short distance away. Chinniah was profoundly happy with his new status. He appreciated the fact that at last he had his own home and a very young bride to share it with. Life seemed to take on new meaning for him. He was a gentle and caring man, and he took great care of his young wife, making sure she wanted for nothing. Their peaceful existence was soon to be changed. Two years later Lutchmi, a beautiful daughter arrived on the scene. Her name meant good fortune. Parenthood elevated Yenkamah to Ama and Chinniah to Nainah.

The family lived in Estcourt for ten years, and three more daughters were added to the family. I was the fourth daughter. When Nainah's next building contract was in Lidgetton, about fifty miles away, he refused to go unless his whole family went with him. I was just a year old when we moved. Ouwa and Thatha were now left alone in Estcourt as all their children had gone to work elsewhere.

We did not stay in Lidgetton for very long as Nainah's next contract was in Nottingham Road. He loved his job, so we all moved again. Nainah's expertise as a builder gave him the opportunity to construct several buildings that still adorn certain parts of Estcourt. He was adept at building with rough stone. As I pass through the centre of the town now, I revel in the pleasure of knowing that my father contributed to the architecture of this advancing place. It was once just a town where two streets ran parallel to each other, and horse-drawn carts and a few cars and bicycles were the only vehicles on the quiet streets. But all that has changed now, only memories cast in stone remain.

My coming-of-age ceremony

Neeli Govender

Neeli Govender, whose real name is Neelaveni (meaning 'blue'), was born in 1974 in Durban. She trained as a librarian at the M L Sultan Technikon in Durban and came to work at one of the museums in Pietermarizburg in 1997, prior to her marriage in 1998. The ceremony she describes here is a traditional Tamil rite of passage, still performed in many families.

I was playing hopscotch in the shade of the big tree in the playground when one of the girls watching said, 'Do you know that when you've got *it* you mustn't go near boys or else you'll get a baby.'

'What's *it*?' I asked.

'Don't you know? Don't you get *it*, you know, periods, when you bleed *down there?* Then you're a big lady and can get married.'

The thought of boys, getting married, and having babies was very far away from my mind at that stage, and I thought that won't happen to me for a very long time.

We knew that sex was an extremely 'secret' subject; we never heard our parents talking about it. We had this funny notion that if our parents had three children, then they had only done it three times, and those parents who had four children had been more naughty than ours because they had done it four times. Because there was so much secrecy, there were a lot of stories made up about it. I would rather have liked to hear about this so-called curse from my mum, but she couldn't talk about it. There were these Health Department nurses who used to come to the school, and we heard about it from them. They had a big chart and they would stand up in front of the girls and point with a long ruler and say, 'See, inside your body you have these two tubes that produce eggs, and every month when your egg is not fertilised it comes down ...' So it was very clinical, and I guess part of me wished this would take a long time before it happened. We first heard about this in about Standard 3. And we girls talked about it and said, 'Shame, it must be something so terrible, and you get sick. You have to say you are sick when it happens.'

I went home one day and I told my mum that the nurses came today and said we must tell our mums about the secret that we learned about today. We were not allowed to talk about this to boys or men, only girls could talk about it. So my mum was aware that I knew about periods, and she probably thought that the nurses had done their job so she didn't have to say anything more. I was very glad that I was one of the girls who didn't get *it*.

But the next year, 1985, when I was eleven and in Standard 4, I got chicken pox and had to stay at home for some time, and just as I was getting better,

 22

on the morning of 22 July, *it* arrived. I was very scared, and I thought: 'Is this what *it* is like?' I went to tell my mum, saying, 'I think I am a big girl now', and she asked, 'Are you quite sure?' And then she had to call the other two aunties who lived with us in our extended family, and they came and had an inspection, which was very embarrassing, particularly as there was much giggling. These two older ladies then had to give me a cleansing bath with turmeric in the water. Also, I was rather upset because all the clothes I had been wearing had to be got rid of, and they were new things that I particularly liked.

Then they dressed me in new clothes, put some of mum's jewellery on me, and a red dot on my forehead. They combed my hair for me, and I began to feel that I looked very pretty. Later a special meal was cooked for me: green beans and a potato curry with *dhal*, which is one of my favourite meals. I remember suddenly feeling very special as I was being treated like a goddess, Lakshmi herself. They made a great fuss of me. I had to stay in my room where only women and girls were allowed, and I thought to myself: 'Wow, this isn't so bad; I'm being treated as a big person.' My father and male relatives were not to see me, and I was told that if they did I would develop lots of pimples.

But, at the same time, I felt very confused because the nurses at school had said this is a secret and you must not talk about it, but here was my mom phoning all her women relatives and friends and telling them about Neeli being a big girl. Why was it that such a secret, dirty thing should be made so public and the cause of so much rejoicing? Also, some members of the family, including my father, went to the temple to tell the priest that I had come of age. They wanted to check whether this had happened at an auspicious time for me. In fact, I don't think that it was an auspicious time, as I was told that a prayer had been said by the priest to ward off any bad luck that might come my way. Because I'm part of the Tamil tradition, a special prayer had to be done to bless and mark this new time in my life. And I thought, 'Oh, why do all these men need to know about what has happened to me – the priest, my father, my uncles? Does the whole world have to know? This is supposed to be secret.'

23

For that whole week I was a mini goddess. My mom's brother (my *mama*), another man, had to bring his wife (my *ather*) and kids to come to visit me, and she had to prepare special food for me and bring it to me. That was nice. What I didn't like was the food I had to drink every morning, which was raw egg and milk mixed with vanilla essence, I think to hide the taste.

A date at the end of that week was set for the big special prayer that had to be done for me. My uncle wanted to set up a tent in the front garden for the ceremony and I thought I would die of embarrassment. All the boys at my school would see it and want to know what had happened to me; this terrible thing that happens to ladies. Thankfully, they decided against the tent. It was to be held in the back yard. There was a lot of excitement about the whole ceremony. Everyone was discussing what was going to happen, and in what order, and who would do what, and I remember thinking, 'Why doesn't anybody ask me what I want?' I made up my mind then that many years later when I got married I would make my own decisions about what I wanted. I did feel excited about what was to happen, and I was thrilled at all the presents that aunts and cousins began to bring for me, things like saris and dresses. My great granny, who was still alive then, with her very small pension brought me a two rand note, which seemed like a lot of money in those days.

In the end I really enjoyed the function which, being held at the back of the house, could not be seen by the neighbours and others. That morning I had to start with a special bath. Then I was dressed in a beautiful blue sari that my granny had brought back from one of her many trips to India and had given to me for this occasion. My aunt did my hair as though I was a little bride. Then my smaller *mama's* wife (my *ather*) led me to the low stool on which I had to sit, just like a bride, and I felt very shy when people said, 'I wonder when the groom is coming?' I still did not think about boys like that, they were another world, so it was uncomfortable for me. A lot of photographs were then taken, which helped to make me think again, 'This isn't too bad.'

All my parents' relatives were there, the whole extended family, the women dressed in their best and most colourful saris. In front of where I sat my mum had

 24

placed the Lakshmi lamp from the house and a tray of fruit, sweetmeats and incense as offerings to the goddess. Many of the women guests then came forward and sprinkled rose water over my head, I think to get rid of any bad luck. I had a little girl sit next to me as my 'attendant'. Each married lady at the ceremony came and stood in front of me to bless me by putting a mixture of turmeric and spices from a tray onto their hands and wiping this on my face, and then putting a red dot on my forehead. The little attendant then handed me a small parcel containing sweets, betel nut and betel leaf, which my mum had prepared and which I gave to each lady. The unmarried girls took a coin which they turned clockwise in front of my face. These coins were then put in a *choombu*, a small brass pot, and later given to charity.

Finally, after the ceremony, a fabulous big feast with lots of lovely food was enjoyed by all, and there were more gifts for me – more clothing (some from Woolworths, which I loved), jewellery boxes, perfumes, bracelets and trinkets.

When I eventually went back to school, somebody who had heard about this thing that had happened at our house spoke about it and some kids asked me about it, and I said, 'No, no, it was nothing, just another prayer that we had at home.' I did everything I could to keep it quiet as I didn't want anybody to know that I was now getting *it* every month.

But far more happened during that time than just the ceremony. Because I wasn't allowed out of my room for those several days, I complained to my mum that I was bored and didn't have anything nice to do and she brought me lots of things to read. As well as a little pamphlet called *What Every Girl Should Know* produced by Lillets, I was introduced to the world of books, reading for the first time *Alice in Wonderland* and *Little Women*, which have remained favourites. These books transported me out of the confines of my room and took me to all sorts of exciting places I could never have imagined. When I went back to school I couldn't stay out of the library, and volunteered to be a library monitor so I could spend as much time as possible in there with the books.

And that's why, when I left school, I went to train as a librarian and have had so much enjoyment from all my various jobs. So much happened to me in that one week when I became a big girl, a woman.

25

The men in my life

Bunny Bhoola

Bunny Maharaj Bhoola was born in 1955 into the Hindi-speaking community of Plessislaer. Her first name is Gumthee, but she has been called Bunny since, as a very small girl, she spent so much time playing with the pet rabbits in the garden of their home. Like other Indian people brought up in the Plessislaer area, she has extremely happy memories of her childhood and the pleasant, supportive community life there. She is the proprietor of African Link Travel and Tours in central Pietermaritzburg, which in March 2003 won an award as an Impumelelo Top 300 empowerment company, bestowed by the Department of Trade and Industry.

My upbringing, when I reflect on it, was a very strange upbringing for a typical traditional Indian family. My grandfather and father were involved in business, and their line of business was undertaking. They ran the Edendale Funeral Furnishers. My father got my sister and me involved in the business while we were still at school. The day I received my driver's licence, my father didn't hesitate to say, 'Take the hearse and go and pick up the coffin.' When I reflect on that now, I think, what a marvellous man! Between my sister and me, we drove many important people to the crematorium and we were considered quite celebrities at that time. We were dropped off at school in hearses every day. Everyone in Edendale knew us. My father had impeccable taste when it came to dressing. We had to dress the part, with our black evening suits, white shirts, black ties and white gloves. We had to stand by the back of the hearse and open the door for the coffin to be lifted out. When a very prominent person died, and my sister was attending, someone thought she was a boy, and later this marriage proposal arrived at the house for her. I also remember we had a very close family member who died, and my father got my sister and me to go into the mortuary to pick up the body. When we saw this old granny of ours, we literally froze, and although we tried carefully to keep the body on the stretcher, her head swung out, and for days on end we didn't sleep, just thinking about it.

But we never questioned our ability as females to do this kind of work. On reflection I realise that this was my foundation, and that this is why I am not intimidated by anything. There were no barriers for us. We grew up with the mortuary in the garage and coffins all around us. My father ordered new hearses from Cape Town, those limousines that were converted to hearses, and we drove down to fetch them. We were only eighteen and nineteen at the time, and we two girls drove these hearses all the way back from Cape Town. This was my introduction into the business field; the strangest introduction that one could possibly have. So, at the tender age of eighteen and nineteen, we were in the crematorium seeing bodies being put into the incinerator, and we accepted this as a normal part of life.

My father never allowed us to live with barriers just because we were girls. As children we were able to do anything we wanted to, within reason. We were not especially protected as girls. I think back on how we used to take our bicycles and ride all over Edendale, or take the bus and go to the movies in Edendale or in town, after seven at night. He never mollycoddled us. We saw *Shaka Zulu*, and we sang 'Tula, tula …' for weeks afterwards. And we mostly saw karate movies because people in the community liked action movies. It was a very free society in which one could feel very comfortable and safe walking down the road, even at ten at night. We were very privileged to be brought up in such a society.

My sister and I were born into the business world and grew up in business. We had a huge orchard and, at six or seven years old, we would pick the fruit, put it on plates, and take it to Edendale Hospital where we stood and sold peaches for one or two cents to people visiting their families. We loved competing with the other vendors. Then we collected the money together and would have a huge bubblegum and cooldrink party.

Later my father bought coaches and we went into the transport business, Maharaj's Coaches. And my sister and I were involved in cashing up at the office in Caluza Road, and would go on our own in the cars to do this and the banking. Sometimes we were tempted to wonder whether my father lacked manpower and knew he could use us as cheap labour, but deep down we knew he had this incredible vision that there was no real distinction between male and female. This was very different to the way in which other parts of my family brought up their girls. There were these gentle, beautiful girls, and at times we envied them like hell, as we thought we were being slave driven. But I have realised with time that he was a wonderful person. Even my mum – she didn't force us into the kitchen at all, and she's the strength in our family.

Edendale was an environment that was very conducive to people growing up happily there; there was no difference between Black families and Indian families. Everyone was a child of the community, and there was an interest in each person's child. People shared the joy and the pain of life.

29

And I experienced that again so strongly when my husband was shot; the Edendale community just rallied around. It was incredible.

After my matric I went to the M L Sultan Technical College in Durban to train as a hairdresser, and then I did my apprenticeship in Lenasia in Johannesburg. I came back to Edendale where I got married in 1979 to Rouhit Bhoola. We lived on a smallholding at Foxhill where we grew vegetables, the biggest cabbages you ever saw, and marigold flowers, and raised chickens. My husband's family – the Bhoolas – were also in business, owning the Machibise Cash Store, which the locals referred to as the Daya Supermarket. They had been in this business for over fifty years. They were like a household name there and they cared for the local community.

In 1991 violence was getting bad in the area. People were fed up with the system, and there was much unrest. My mother-in-law lived with my brothers-in-law and there were several attempted break-ins at night, so they decided to relocate to Mountain Rise. My mother-in-law did not want to move as she had lived there since she was eleven, and that was home to her, and she still yearns for the place. And our families had not moved out when the others did in the Group Areas removals because we were some of the oldest business people there. We were very resistant to the move, and we just stayed on.

There were two shootings before the fatal attack. People tried to rob the business, to steal from the shop. My husband was in the dispatch section of the shop, so he was the most exposed. The first time they shot at my husband the bullet whizzed past his head, and on the second occasion the bullet hit him in the thumb. He came home with a bandage, and I laughed at him, 'Ag, man, shame!' and joked about the whole thing because in my mind he was such a super strong human being.

But strangely, shortly after that something inside me began to feel very turbulent. I began to approach his brothers about moving out of the area, and I began to argue with my husband to move. I even drove all the way to Durban to try to persuade one of his uncles to urge him to go. I felt that there was an urgency in me to try to get him out, and this was totally unlike me.

30

I recall very clearly – I had a hairdressing salon in town, my own business, in Church Street at that time, and it was Friday the 6th of December. I was blow-drying a very good friend's hair and, in the midst of this, I became overwhelmed by thinking of my husband. I couldn't understand it, but my mind became totally unhinged. I even switched the hairdryer off and told my friend, 'There's something strange happening. I'm thinking about my husband so much, and I'll call him as soon as I finish your hair.'

And then the phone rang and my brother said, 'You have to get to the hospital.' I rushed with my sister to the hospital. I recall that I was dressed like a real tart. I had this short skirt on, you know, this huge hair style, very Afro and modern, a woman of the nineties, with big earrings, and I walked into the hospital with these high-heeled shoes, announcing who I was, and that I had come to see my husband. And the doctor came and said, 'Come with me; you need to sit down. I need to talk to you.' Then he told me that my husband had died and it just didn't register. It didn't register for weeks.

For a highly confident person like myself to just go off the rails … I just stopped functioning. I became oblivious of my two children. The communities in Edendale and Maritzburg are totally responsible for what I am today because they cradled me through my grief. Black, White, Indian – everyone. They cried with me, they prayed for me. I just couldn't accept it until very recently and, to be honest, I still feel his presence. I mix with lots of men but there's no appeal for me at all – their noses are too big, there's hair growing out of their ears … He was my soul mate and he has guided me to where I am today. From what I have gathered, the moment when I thought of him at work that day was exactly the time he was shot. So there must have been some kind of telepathy between us. It's something I've never experienced before in my life, but I have learnt that one does have these strange experiences.

The loss, and not being in control of your senses, is devastating – you slip into another make-believe world, and you have no control over your actions or your life. And I marvel at other women who have experienced similar traumas, alone in strange countries; how do they manage? I had the whole community, and still

31

I was a doofy. It's been a long road, it's been a very painful road, but I believe that is what life is about: learning lessons, and I'm very grateful that God let me meet someone who allowed me to develop, gave me enough freedom as an Indian woman, never doubted me. And I feel that between the two men, my father and my husband, they encouraged me towards the path that I am now on.

My husband and I were both business people and, when I was running my hairdressing salon, he would encourage me and my ideas, and participate in the hairdressing shows. My encounters with the men in my life have been so good; I've been blessed. And I think my son has similar qualities, and I think 'Wow, am I lucky!'

The shooting in which my husband was killed just destroyed his family. Pretty well overnight, they simply packed up and left and went to live in Mountain Rise and opened small businesses in town. My husband's brothers have become like old men who often sit together and yearn for the days that have gone. They are still a very important part of my life and the children's lives. But they never thought a person from the local community would ever do something like that to their family because they grew up with all these people. The police caught two young boys, eighteen and nineteen, and I went in there to see them with so much anger. And I looked at these two children and thought they must have got such a terrible shock when they shot my husband; they didn't even take a bubble gum, they just ran. So, I believe that my husband and these two boys were just victims of circumstance.

And now I'm in tourism, and I think I was meant for tourism. I also think there would have been no place for my husband in this life of mine, so in the greater scheme I was meant to open other doors. I would not have been a good wife now if he was around; it takes up so much of my time. I am so grateful that after so much pain, I have my life back again. Very few women can say that they are in total control of their destiny. I have become more spiritual through all this, and think that I would have become very materialistic if I had not changed. Being on my own, I'm trying to rise to a higher plain and make peace with my Maker, and I'm moving more to the Arya Samaj. Their simple way of praying has attracted me very much.

 32

God works in strange ways. On the Monday after my husband died, my neighbour in Foxhill told me that our properties were going to be expropriated by the government. Within three days I had the letter informing me of this, and within six months the whole place was sold, and I got a good price that allowed me to buy a new place, and move. So I lost in one way, but many other doors opened for me. Another very strange thing happened too. There was a cottage that my husband used to drive past in Prince Alfred Street and admire, and say, 'I'd like to buy that house one day.' That is the house I bought, and I never planned to buy it, and that's where I live now. It has been an amazing journey, it really has.

33

How I became a Hindu priest

Vidya Satgoor

Vidya Satgoor was born in 1936 in Grey's Hospital and grew up in Plessislaer, just outside Pietermaritzburg, where her parents had lived all their lives. She went to Sutherlands Primary School and then to the Indian Girls' High School in Berg Street in Pietermaritzburg, where she matriculated. Thereafter she trained as a teacher and taught for twenty years before deciding that what she really wanted to do was serve her community by becoming a priest in the Arya Samaj (Society of the Righteous), a Neo- or reformed Hindu group which is unusual in that it accepts women as priests.

Looking back, I realise how lucky I was that my father was a very religious person and a Vedic priest, so he made sure we all sat every evening to recite our prayers, and if we didn't attend prayers then we got no supper. Every Sunday we all had to go to the hall for service in the early morning before breakfast, and there was no breakfast for those who didn't get up to go. My mum, too, shared this interest in religion, and she was the first President of the Plessislaer Stree Samaj for women. So we learnt all the Vedic *mantras* from an early age.

All my grandparents came from India: my *dada* (father's father) was Hindi-speaking from Uttar Pradesh, an imposing, very traditional figure, who worked on the railways in Pietermaritzburg and wore a turban and a huge handlebar moustache till the day he died; and my *dadi* (father's mother) who, with her brother, was kidnapped from the streets of Calcutta when she was about eight and brought on a ship to South Africa. Later she met my grandfather and they married when they were very young and went to live in Plessislaer. My *dadi* helped to support the family with her hawking, and only stopped when her children were grown up and earning enough money. Later my father did some research and went to visit the village outside Calcutta where she and her brother came from and found some of their relatives still there. One of my earliest memories is of going to the station at Mason's Mill in the afternoons to meet her as she came off the train from her day's hawking of vegetables from our market garden in the city, in West and Pine streets. She carried two large baskets, one on her head and the other over her arm, and we would help her carry the baskets home. Everyone called her 'Mary'. She was a strong, beautiful woman, and all of us eight grandchildren loved her dearly.

My father and his brother were teachers, and as soon as they had saved sufficient money they both built large brick houses to replace the small hut in which they and their sister had been brought up by their parents. Later my father became a school principal, and he also did extra teaching at the Natal Tech to earn more money. Our house was very large, and I remember my father buying a big Falkirk stove, and a geyser for hot water, so that we were very comfortable. In the yard there was a well for water, which meant that we were able to grow and eat from our

 36

large vegetable garden. My father was a keen gardener and encouraged us all to go into the garden to help. We also had poultry and a cow for milk, and before we had a car we used to go into town in our horse and cart to shop on Saturdays.

Plessislaer was a very beautiful place with green hills, and a very united, happy community in those days, with Indians and Blacks living close together in harmony, and all the children playing together. We all spoke Zulu fluently, and the doors of our house were always open as there was no fear of crime. We always moved about perfectly freely and safely over the whole district. Of course, all that changed when the Group Areas Act moved all the Indians out, but we all have such happy memories of our life there.

When my younger sister, Githa, left for India to study medicine, almost the whole of the Plessislaer Indian community travelled down to Durban to see her off at the docks.

When I went to high school, my older brother used to travel by bus with me every day into Maritzburg and drop me off at the school gate, then go on to his school in Woodlands, and come back to fetch me in the afternoon to return home on the bus, after which we still had to walk a long distance to get home. It was a long journey and a very long day. But we enjoyed our studies and worked hard.

After training as a teacher, my first appointment was at Mount Partridge which I enjoyed very much. It was through teaching that I met my husband, as he was also a teacher. We got married in 1958, and it was one of the largest weddings the district had ever seen, with over a thousand guests. What a wonderful wedding! Then I moved into town to live with my husband's family, and we both continued to teach and to bring up our family.

After teaching for about twenty years, I felt increasingly unsettled and became more and more convinced that I had a calling to do religious work. I had always been a very regular attender at services, and felt the need to do more studying of my faith. Also, I was becoming more and more involved in propagating the Arya Samaj teachings, so that I felt the time had come for me to put my energies into my religious work rather than school teaching. My father was very encouraging because he was a Vedic priest, and he said if this is what I feel called to do then

I must follow it through. So I started studying to become an Arya Samaj priest in this reformed Hindu movement founded by Swami Dayanand Saraswati in India in 1875, in order to bring Hindus 'back to the Vedas' and the truths taught in these scriptures.

First, I embarked on learning Hindi up to matric level. Having completed that and passed all the exams, I started on an intensive three-year course learning the various religious practices and rituals. For this I had to learn Sanskrit, to understand and be able to recite the religious rituals. This was quite a challenge, but one that I enjoyed. At first I studied locally under two *pundits*, and then for the last year I had to travel down to Durban every week to be tutored by Pundit Nardev Vedalankar. Finally, we had to take an oral as well as a written exam, both of which I passed, and then I was ordained in 1988. The ceremony was held at the beautiful, big Vedic Temple in Carlisle Street in Durban, and consisted of a *Maha Yajna* (Great Fire ritual) conducted by Pundit Nardev where all of us five new women priests recited *mantras* and took vows to serve the community and to promote the Vedic teachings of the Arya Samaj for the spiritual, moral and social betterment of Hindus.

 38

I am now the priest at the Raisethorpe Arya Samaj, which means a service every Sunday as well as Hindi school for adults every Tuesday and Wednesday, and song practices where we teach new *bhajans*. There is also a Vedic culture class where a group comes to study and discuss the Vedic scriptures, particularly the *Bhagavad Gita* and the *Ramayana*, and learn about the meaning of various rituals, particularly the *Yajna* and *Havan* fire ceremony. We see this ancient Vedic fire ceremony as central to our worship. We are not fire worshippers, but promote the symbolism of fire as enlightening, able to dispel the darkness of ignorance and evil, both within and without a person. Offerings of grains, *ghee, samagree* and camphor are thrown into the flames, to produce an aromatic scent and as a symbol of purifying our surroundings and bringing a sense of unity and harmony to participants. People also make offerings of money, which is given away to charity. We do not believe in the necessity for idols to represent God, who we regard as One, Supreme Creator, formless, almighty and changeless, neither male nor female. God is referred to as *Paramathma*

(Greatest Soul) and is represented only by the *Om* symbol. So we urge people not to worship idols, although we don't criticise anyone who does.

Another thing that I enjoy doing is giving educational talks to various groups, explaining the meaning of religious festivals such as *Divali, Shivarathri, Holi*, as well as the importance and meaning of the various life rituals (*Samskaras*) such as birth, naming the child, removing the first hair, when the child first goes to school, the three threads coming-of-age ceremony for boys and girls, weddings and funerals.

Quite a lot of my work is done at the Sunrise Senior Citizens Club because the old people often feel insecure and frequently fall ill, so they need prayers for health and prosperity. They are really appreciative of what I do there.

If I am called out to someone who is dying, I will always go to offer prayers of comfort and for them to be released from their suffering, for God to take them. The Aryan prayer book sets out some very comforting prayers to be recited at funerals. Members of the family are reminded that the spirit has no beginning or end, is never born and never dies.

I have many weddings too, which are very enjoyable. We also frequently participate in Hindi eisteddfods, where I help to prepare participants to recite from the scriptures, the *Ramayana, Bhagavad Gita*, sing Hindi songs, and perform a Hindi play.

Much of my work as a priest involves counselling people with problems, particularly family problems. People often come to my house here and I speak to them and try to sort out what is wrong, and bring the family together again. Unfortunately, in male-dominated homes where the wife is subservient and is expected to serve her husband continually, there is much unhappiness, and the children suffer from this as well. Often the husband does not give his wife enough money to run the home. Even when the wife also goes out to work, she is expected to come home, do all the cooking, washing up and cleaning, while the husband just throws off his shoes, puts his feet up and watches TV. Wife beating is very common and alcoholism is a major problem, particularly among the men, and many men have affairs. The Arya Samaj teaches that there should be equality

39

between men and women, that there should be respect for each other, and that work should be shared, so I have to try to get this message through to them, which isn't always easy, but some do begin to try to practise it. But many of the boys have been brought up to treat women as servants and leave all the work to them. Their mothers encourage it because they believe that women have got to be subservient to the men. I say, 'Come on, let's share the work; my husband and sons help with housework.' People need to learn that times are changing and, after all, most of us are not still sitting in *purdah*, so we've got to move with the times.

The very fact that the Arya Samaj ordains women as priests shows how different it is from the ancient traditional Hinduism, which never allows women to become priests. Swami Dayanand taught that both women and men should be educated and encouraged to study the scriptures in the holy language of Sanskrit in order to participate in religious rituals in the *mandirs*. He emphasised that women are not unclean, even when they are menstruating. This is a natural, God-given function and should never exclude women from participating in *havan* and other rituals. We just don't make an issue about menstruation.

40

Since the 1980s when it was started, the South African Arya Samaj community has ordained more women priests than is done in India, which is something we are proud of. The local Arya Samaj community generally has a more enlightened attitude towards male and female relationships than the rest of Hinduism.

In the Hindu community, weddings and funerals are the two most important *samskaras*, life cycle rituals. Particularly with weddings, I try to do some counselling about the meaning of the rituals and their symbolism, and how the marriage relationship is all about give and take, sharing responsibility, having respect for each other, commitment and understanding. The wedding ceremony is elaborate and very colourful with lots of symbolism, so all the way through I explain what is happening and what it means, and guide the couple through the various rituals. Young couples are usually dressed in their wonderful traditional wedding finery, and are often quite nervous, so I try to reassure and encourage them. When it comes to the vows, I ask all present to think back on their own weddings and to renew their vows while the young couple are taking theirs.

One of the current problems we have with Hinduism here is that there has been a mushrooming of a great many new groups, which has caused people to become 'religious shoppers'. They come one week to our service, and then the next week they go to the Sai service, and then to the Divine Life Society, and then come back to us, looking to see where they can get peace. Many people just seem to want to be 'happy clappers', merely singing *bhajans* and clapping, without very much challenge. So, many of the people who come to our services are not staunch Arya Samaj people and are not really committed to anything, but I always try to find time to talk to them and see how I can help them.

I am one of eight women Arya Samaj priests in Maritzburg, and most functions are performed by women rather than men priests. We are generally more popular with the people as they view us as more progressive than the men, performing the rituals more efficiently and clearly. And, with family problems, we are seen as more understanding, caring and compassionate.

I really love all my work, and am kept very busy with all the various aspects of it. Luckily I've got a loud voice, so I can recite my *mantra*s very clearly, and I believe in always giving an explanation of what I am doing, and people like that. I take my responsibilities in the community very seriously. People look to me as a leader, one who can guide them on the right path, so I believe I have to be a role model for them.

41

Madame Ambassadrice

Rabia Motala

Rabia Motala was born in Kokstad in East Griqualand in 1932 where, although there were no other Indians there at that time, her grandfather had established a shop in the 1880s. She was sent to school in Durban until she was thirteen years old, and then helped her father in his shop. At the age of 19 she married a newly qualified medical doctor, Mohammed (Chota) Motala, and went to live with him in Pietermaritzburg where they became deeply involved in anti-apartheid politics. Many of the central figures in the anti-apartheid struggle, such as Chief Albert Luthuli, Nelson Mandela and Walter Sisulu, came to stay in their home. They had numerous night-time visits from the Security Police and Rabia's husband was detained on several occasions, the longest spell being for 150 days. Later he was banned for five years. During these years, Rabia found time to complete her matric and to enrol at UNISA for a BA degree, as well as to serve on the SA Peace Council and the Banishees Committee. After the first democratic elections in 1994, the Motalas were sent to Morocco as the first South African ambassadorial couple to that country.

Our Moroccan adventure began when we left Jan Smuts Airport in Johannesburg for that exotic country towards the end of 1996, summer time. We were taken to the VIP lounge at the airport and were seated in unexpected comfort while we waited for our flight. This was a real eye-opener to me, and just the beginning of an exciting and wonderful new experience for both of us. On many occasions during the apartheid era we had applied for travel permits and passports and had always been refused, and here we were travelling in luxury to take up an important post in a foreign country.

Towards the end of 1989 we had received a message from the Security Police conveying a request from Mr Nelson Mandela that we visit him in the Victor Verster prison where he was then being held. It was the best thing that had happened to us for many years. We went in great excitement and the eight hours we spent with him that day were among the happiest we had ever experienced.

 44

With the unbanning of the ANC in 1990, an ANC branch was established in our area and we joined, with many others. This was a totally new experience, things were changing, and my husband's political activities now continued in a different guise.

Then, at a mass meeting in the Pietermaritzburg City Hall in 1996, President Mandela announced his decision to appoint my husband as an ambassador to a foreign country. When Morocco was offered, my husband happily accepted.

On our arrival in Casablanca, we were again led to the VIP lounge and met by many dignitaries, the foreign minister, and other high-ranking government officials, who were all most hospitable, serving us sweet mint tea and other welcoming refreshments. Some South African staff from the Trade Mission were also present, the administrative secretary and the political secretary, a Mr de Villiers and a Mr Kok respectively, and their wives. It was lovely to see them and to converse in English, while most people around us were speaking French. The Moroccans were overjoyed to have an ambassador from President Mandela's country to establish the first ever South African Embassy there.

About an hour's drive took us further up the coast to Rabat, the capital, Morocco's second largest city after Casablanca, and situated on the Oued Bou Regreg estuary, once used as a port by the Phoenicians. The river separates the old city of Sale from Rabat. In Rabat we were accommodated in a hotel for the night before being taken to our beautiful residence the next morning. The house was wonderful, with antique furniture, five bedrooms, three lounges, a large dining room, and the most beautiful cutlery and crockery for use on official occasions. Anni Kok, the political secretary's wife, was so wonderful and kind, and such a great help. I had no previous experience of diplomatic protocol and she showed me the ropes and explained much of the quite complicated formalities that had to be observed on various occasions.

Rabat as a city greatly impressed us with its clean, neat and well-organised atmosphere, with many exceptionally attractive public buildings, the old and the new side by side. It is a most pleasant place in which to live. We were shown around and taken to visit the Medina, the ancient walled quarter of the city with its narrow, crowded alleyways, some of which dates back to the twelfth century. There is an ancient and beautiful mosque there, which housed one of the earliest *madrassas* where students studied sciences almost a thousand years ago. We watched with fascination some of the thousands of craftspeople who live and work in the colourful *souks* of the Medina, crafting goods from metal, wood and leather, and creating ceramic work for sale to locals and tourists. There were amazingly delicately carved wooden dishes and stools, tooled leather purses, handbags, belts and slippers (*babouches*) dyed bright greens, reds, blues and yellows, wonderful handwoven carpets, filigree silver earrings, bracelets and pendants, all a delight to the eyes. Moroccans are very fond of gardens and trees, cool green spaces with colourfully tiled fountains. Running through the new city is a beautiful wide avenue lined with ornamental orange trees whose blossoms scent the streets in spring.

Morocco, like other third world countries, has its share of large numbers of poor people and the problems that poverty brings. It is just as well that there are tens of thousands of self-employed craftspeople in every large city. They all have skills passed on from one generation to another, over hundreds of years, and the products they make and sell help significantly in reducing the number of unemployed.

45

Settling down in a foreign country brought with it the problem of language. In Morocco, while Arabic is the state language, French is most commonly spoken. There are those in commerce who speak English, as do the well-educated people, but – to our astonishment – all the West African diplomats were French-speaking. Even though we had undergone some French tuition at the Foreign Affairs Department, this proved to be inadequate. Of course, at the Embassy the locally recruited staff were competent in English, but it took a few months before we felt comfortable language-wise.

It was a source of great happiness and stimulation to us that we were now exposed not only to North Africa but also to much of the Middle East as well as to the large number of diplomatic missions from countries in the rest of Africa, Europe, the Americas and Asia.

Initially I felt rather homesick because I like people and not being able to converse with many people made me feel quite lonely at times. But gradually I got to know more and more people who spoke English and began to make some friends and to feel more at home. The wife of the Malaysian ambassador, Farida, was to become one of my closest friends.

There are a great many duties allocated to the wife of an ambassador. I was addressed as Madame Ambassadrice and, as a representative of my country, was expected to promote a good image of the country. There were many formal social functions that were entirely my responsibility, and all these had their own series of protocols to be observed. I had to learn who was who, and who was more senior to whom, and how to seat guests at the dinner table. There was a table plan, setting out where everyone had to sit. The most important lady had to sit on my husband's right, and the most important man had to sit on my right, all according to rank. There were waiters to serve the food and, once you were seated with your guests, there was no getting up and running through to the kitchen to check on anything; you just had to remain seated and allow the staff to cope. We were also expected to have fresh flowers in all the entertaining rooms, even in the bathroom and the loo.

It is mandatory for all wives of ambassadors to join the *Cercle Diplomatique*, which met once monthly to exchange ideas and arrange functions. Contributions to local welfare organisations providing assistance to the sick, the poor and the disabled had to be made through the *Cercle Diplomatique*.

The national days of all countries have to be observed and celebrated, and each embassy has to arrange its own function. This entails preparations starting at least a month or more in advance. About three hundred people are invited to a social evening where a lavish spread of food and drinks is laid out. No speeches are made on these occasions. Commonwealth Day involved another celebration, with an official dinner hosted by a different Commonwealth country each year.

Moroccans in the cities are highly Westernised and many don't go to mosque every day, but on Fridays all mosques are full. My husband was able to attend a mosque just across from the South African Embassy. People in the country areas tend to attend mosque much more regularly than the city dwellers.

We soon learnt that Moroccans really entertain in a big way. They are passionate about food and preparing lavish dishes and feasts, so we were introduced to a great many new experiences with food. Their traditional food is couscous (steamed semolina), prepared in a variety of ways and usually eaten with vegetables and spicy meat. Being a Mediterranean country, olives are also very popular, with an amazing variety of different sorts. Moroccans are also extremely fond of pastries and honey, almond and sesame cakes. Here in South Africa we serve platters of food arranged flat on the plate, but in Morocco and Middle Eastern countries the food is piled up, pyramid style, whether it be couscous, fruit or wonderful varieties of pastries, often covered in chocolate or other colourful toppings. Mountains of food – and it all looks so very beautiful. Many wealthy Moroccans often prefer to serve French cuisine on special occasions.

I also joined the International Gourmet Group, which gave me experience of cooking from all over the world as each member would hold a dinner made up of a menu of favourite dishes from her country. It was great fun. At the monthly meetings the hostess would do the cooking, with twenty people watching each step of the way. And we then swapped recipes. There were South American, French, Spanish, Pakistani, Lebanese and Indian women, and many of us still keep in touch. I don't think I'm an especially good cook, but I held two meetings

47

while I was there and gave members dishes such as briyani, chicken curry, bobotie and *dhal*, which were very popular. You could be kept busy morning, noon and night in Rabat if you wanted to – there is so much entertaining and social activity going on. In the first few months I put on so much weight that I had to do something about it.

I had very good Moroccan staff who picked up English quite well and taught me some French. They cooked us Moroccan food, but my husband likes Indian food best, so I made sure I brought Indian spices and condiments from South Africa whenever we went home in order to give him his favourite dishes. I taught my Moroccan cook how to do many of the recipes, such as briyani, lentils and rotis, although I did much of the cooking myself, which was considered very unusual. Most women in the diplomatic community did no cooking themselves, but left it all to their staff.

 48 I found it exciting to be able to travel quite a lot and see a great deal of the country, both the rich and the poorer parts. Morocco, which is just about a third of the size of South Africa, offers very striking and varied scenery, from the Mediterranean coast in the north to the Sahara in the south and the Atlas Mountains, all within a few hours drive. We often went to visit Casablanca, a great modern city, and we went as far south as Ouarzazate, towards the Atlas Mountains and the Sahara, and to the sparkling white ancient sea port Essaouira, the harbour lined with old cannons where, we were told, Orson Wells made the movie *Othello*. We also saw Marrakesh, Fez and Tangier, all wonderful old cities with Medinas, some with amazing terracotta buildings, others brilliantly white, many with magnificent blue-, white-, yellow- and brown-coloured tiles and mosaics, imposing pointed arch gateways, and beautiful mosques with unusual square minarets.

As the ambassador's wife, you get a lot of invitations. Our women's groups also did a lot of travelling together in buses, sometimes on day trips and sometimes staying overnight. I went with these groups up north to various cities on the coast and, wherever we went, we were so warmly welcomed, staying in the most beautiful places, being entertained, and often even being given gifts by the people we visited. They were so generous.

One of my best visits away from Morocco was to Dubai on the Arabian Gulf, which is part of the southern Persian Gulf. Here we, the women of the *Cercle Diplomatique*, were invited by the Sheikhah, the wife of the Sheikh Saeed bin Maktoum. She sent the royal plane to take about fifty of us to visit the United Arab Emirates. We flew first to Abu Dhabi, the capital of the Emirates, where we were met in the VIP lounge, which was amazingly opulent. Then we went on to see Dubai, sprawling round a great inlet, the Dubai Creek. From a small pearl diving town it has grown into a thriving cosmopolitan metropolis, in just over fifteen years.

Altogether we were there for ten days, staying at top five-star hotels. Throughout the visit we were treated like royalty, with everything on the house, and we were taken everywhere in a convoy of large cars. They fell over themselves to make us welcome, and we were taken to see much of the country. Twenty-five years ago most of the country was just desert and what they have done there is quite fantastic. It's very clean, very organised, very rich, and incredibly green. They took us to a ladies beach near the city of Dubai, which had excellent facilities for women to swim in privacy and comfort in the warm water with small waves, and we had a feast of a luncheon. Our guides were most interesting women, educated in America – one was a doctor and another an engineer. One evening we went in luxury 4x4s into the desert, driving up and down across the sand dunes which made some of the women feel a bit queasy. But our discomfort was soon forgotten when we arrived at the tent. It was enormous and colourful, cream on the outside but red and blue inside, lit with brightly coloured lanterns and splendid oriental carpets spread over the ground, which created a wonderful atmosphere of warm hospitality. Here we enjoyed yet another feast with the most amazing selection of dishes – grilled crayfish, kebabs, *tajines* piled high, and all sorts of international foods, Eastern and Western. Tons of food! They had also arranged for us to have camel rides, which I can only describe as interesting and different. I felt rather nervous of the animal lurching to its feet, and then sitting so high off the ground. But the camel was very well behaved and we walked around slowly, and I got off safely.

On another evening we were taken round the Creek on a kind of houseboat with a very comfortably furnished lounge and restaurant with beautifully laid tables, groaning with food. The lovely cool breeze, dhows sailing peacefully across the water, and the

49

skyline of the city waterfront with the high-rise buildings outlined with coloured lights is a scene I won't ever forget. We were also invited to attend a royal wedding that was happening at the time, which was also startlingly opulent. It was held in a huge, lavishly decorated hall, the walls completely draped with cream silk and white flowers, with the bride just dripping in diamonds – her wedding gown was studded with dozens and dozens of diamonds. And yet again, the feast that followed was spectacular. Another wonderful experience! The other women on the trip were also highly impressed by everything; we all had an extremely jolly time and I made some nice friends.

My husband was kept very busy with his many official duties and sometimes he had to attend functions hosted by the king. During the fasting month of Ramadan, he had to go to the palace every night with all the other Muslim ambassadors to attend a special session of prayer. This meant that I was often on my own because of his duties, but I always felt safe. I have lived through some lonely times in my life when my husband was detained for political reasons, or when he was away at conferences. It's generally very safe in Morocco, and often in the evening I would enjoy taking a walk. Sometimes the chauffeur would take me shopping to a supermarket where I could choose what I needed, so I moved around on my own quite regularly.

When King Hassan II died in 1999, we really experienced the superb organisation of the Moroccans. The king died on the Friday and had to be buried on the Sunday because, according to Muslim tradition, burial had to take place as soon as possible after his death. Dignitaries from all over the world had to be present – royalty from many countries, people such as Prince Charles, Bill Clinton, Kofi Annan, President Mbeki, and so on. They got it all together for the state funeral on Sunday, and the king was buried in the grand, richly decorated mausoleum close to the South African Embassy where his father is buried. People were very fond of the king and many were extremely upset by his death. Over a million people turned out for the funeral, lining the streets to watch the procession.

We were fortunate to have many visitors from South Africa, which was marvellous. My daughter came twice, and my son too, and other old and special friends from Maritzburg. A number of South Africans, who were not known to us but were visiting Morocco, also popped in from time to time, seeking advice about travel

50

in Morocco. It gave me great pleasure to meet them and to be able to help them. While we were there, President Mandela visited at the invitation of King Hassan II. Arrangements for accommodation were made by the palace, but it was part of the ambassador's duty to be at his call, and my husband and I were to meet him every day. We were highly delighted to see Madiba because he is an old friend and had often stayed with us in Maritzburg during the 1950s before he was imprisoned. We were thrilled to be introduced to Madame Graca, such a distinguished activist, and to have the opportunity of spending many happy hours in her company. I thoroughly enjoyed accompanying Madame Graca, showing her around town and the Medina where she shopped for fabric and gifts for her family back home. She took great pleasure in looking at everything and choosing her purchases very carefully. On one occasion she invited me to lunch with her and the king's daughters. This gave me a lucky opportunity to see the palace, which is not open to the public. It is simply out of this world in its splendour, from the main entrance with its terracotta red walls and shiny green tiles above the ancient arched Bab ar-Rouah, Gate of the Winds, to the great courtyards with their wonderful mosaic-clad fountains and ceilings intricately carved in wood with the most beautiful geometric decorations.

Every year in December we came home for a month, but we looked forward to going back after the break. When it was time to leave, after just over three years, I felt sad as I had grown to like our host country and the wonderful and stimulating time we had experienced with so many new friends. It was strange coming home and settling down to our old lives, after all our experiences in North Africa and the Middle East. We feel very privileged to have had such a unique experience, living abroad away from the tensions and anxieties that had plagued our lives in the past. But now things are different here, and we are free to do the things that were previously denied to us. So now we have time to keep in contact with relatives, children and grandchildren, and friends and comrades with whom we forged bonds during the struggle. But often I can't help thinking sadly of those who did not survive to see freedom.

Struggle days are over, or are they? There is another struggle to be won now: the transformation of our country, which is on course, and the long march to peace and security for all the people of this country.

51

What about the wedding?

Champa Bositsumune

Champa (whose name means magnolia flower) Bositsumune was born in 1956 near Estcourt in the KwaZulu-Natal Midlands and attended school up to Grade 8 at the Estcourt State Indian High School. After her marriage she came to live in Pietermaritzburg where she studied both Hindi and Sanskrit with the Hindi Shiksha Sangh in Durban. She now teaches Hindi to primary school children at the Springhaven Primary School in Northdale. She has written poems, short stories and songs in English, Hindi and Bhojpuri, and is often asked to perform recitals from the Hindu scriptures, the Ramayana *and the* Bhagavad Gita. *This story, in a shorter form, featured as one of the ten finalists in* The Natal Witness *'True Stories of KwaZulu-Natal' competition, and was published in the same newspaper in September 2003. (The surname 'Bositsumune' is a corruption of* Vasishthamuni, *created by a registrar of births.* Vasishtha *is the name of a famous Vedic sage, while* muni *literally means sage or saint.)*

Rensburgdrift. A little settlement in the midlands of KwaZulu-Natal, on the outskirts of Estcourt, en route to Weenen. Did you ever hear of this place?

Many years ago, a small colony of Indians, predominantly Hindu, decided to put down their roots here, surrounded by rocky hills scattered with acacias. There was no river nearby and the grass was always dry. I don't know why, but settle here they did, ready to challenge the hardship of the rural area. They developed the land and built their houses with mud blocks and tin roofs. They had no electricity, so were dependent on lamps and candles. A little distance from their houses, they built pit toilets. Water they got from wells and boreholes. They toiled from morning till night, turning the soil with their oxen and ploughs. Being nationals of India, they were no strangers to agriculture. Soon the barren fields of Rensburgdrift were abundantly blessed with luscious green vegetables, fruit, mealies and sugar cane. These they sold in town to earn a living. They also had cattle for milk as well as poultry, so they ate off the land and were largely self-sufficient. It was a life full of tranquillity.

 54

The colloquial language was Bhojpuri, a dialect of Hindi spoken by the residents of Bhojpur State of north India. Although many of them were illiterate, these people knew very well how to preserve their language, culture and self-esteem.

Arranged marriages were very prevalent in those days. It was a close-knit community. Although not blood relatives, there was a quality of reverence among the people. The elders we called grandmother or grandfather, the younger generation we called uncle and aunt. We children regarded each other as *bhaiya* (brother) or *didi* (sister). In this way, everybody became related. Most families had their own private temple in their backyard. Ours had pictures and images of various deities like Shiva, Ram, Sita, Kali and Sarasvati. *Deepavali* and other festivals were celebrated in grand style. I remember the colourful gatherings on the hill once a year at spring time, when we did *Indra Pooja* (the prayer for the rain god Indra). This was a simple communal prayer in which everybody participated. We paid homage to Mother Nature and asked for her blessings for the new agricultural year. The prayer always ended with *Punditji* (the priest) blowing his conch and everybody paying obeisance to Lord Indra. Sometimes, miraculously, we were blessed on the same day with showers from the heavens.

My father came from one of the pioneer families of Rensburgdrift. Ramdeen by name, they were five brothers and two sisters. The Ramdeen brothers lived in a joint family system. This was a very large family and women shared the household chores, which were done in a very organised manner. In all my childhood I can never remember any sort of family dispute. Those were really happy times. We played three tins, rounders, hopscotch, hide and seek and house-house. We also enjoyed *gulli-danda*, a game of tip cat played with a short stick. I remember my uncle rounding up all the children to go into the fields to help pick vegetables and chillies, and then he would sit right there in the garden and make pickles over an open fire. It was lots of hard work, but great fun.

The nearest school was in Estcourt. In the very early days, only the boys were allowed to attend school. My older girl cousins stayed at home and did what we now jokingly call 'The Household Management Course' under the strict but loving guidance of my grandmother, until their marriages were arranged.

Then came a time when we younger children began growing, and so did the need for bigger living quarters. This was the only reason for the Ramdeen brothers to separate. But they did not go far. The brothers built their houses next to each other on the farm, so as not to break the family ties.

My parents had five children: three girls first, and then two boys. From an early age, Father inculcated good family values in us. Every Sunday morning we gathered on our big verandah for Sunday service. We sang *bhajans* and listened to talks on our scriptures. Sometimes we took part in rallies in town at which were presented items such as sketches, songs and dances. Times were changing fast, though. After the demise of Grandmother, and Father's gentle intervention, we younger girls were lucky enough to have some schooling. I went to school when I was about six and stayed till Standard 8.

One not so happy incident I remember was when I was in Standard 2 and over the weekend we went for a picnic at the Wagondrift Dam. There were swings there and we wanted to play on them, but there was a notice saying 'Whites only', so we weren't allowed to. But we made up our own games and rolled in the grass and had fun in spite of that.

55

When the girls came to what was called 'marriageable age', they were taken out of school and their marriages were arranged. A year or so after my older sister's wedding, Mother thought that it was time for me to marry. But I had a bit of a rebellious spirit in me. I was not too happy with arranged marriages and I told my parents so. Not that I had a secret boyfriend or anything like that. No, on the contrary, I was happy with my schooling and bringing home good results. However, I did have numerous proposals, but I continually said, No, No, No!

So, my younger sister had to leave school and get married before me. At that time, Father's health was failing. After many talks and arguments with Mother, I finally gave in. I did not complete Standard 8. My marriage was also arranged. A family friend in Maritzburg said she knew a very nice boy, her nephew, who she could introduce to me, so she acted as the *arguwa,* the one who negotiates marriage connections.

 56

He did not come on the traditional white stallion. In fact, he came in a white mini, together with his parents and the *arguwa.* They were all from Maritzburg. He was very handsome with his longish hair and a gorgeous moustache. I was dressed up in the first sari I had ever worn and, after tea and sweetmeats had been served, we were left alone to talk. We were both very shy and didn't know what to talk about, so tried to make awkward small talk. But to cut a long story short: 'They came, they saw, and they liked.' So when the elders came back in we said 'Yes'.

The marriage date was set for about a year ahead, in 1976, and nearly every weekend Suren came courting on the farm. We had quite a lot in common. We were both shy, both from Bhojpuri communities, and both devout young people, so we got to know each other better. We had just less than a year to prepare for the big day. Mother took charge of all the wedding preparations, from guest lists and invitations to clothing for the family and my trousseau. Father was getting weaker by the day. The help we got from my uncles and aunts was remarkable. While the menfolk painted the house and did whatever had to be done outside, the womenfolk spring-cleaned inside. The whole place was abuzz with joyful activity. They drank *caay* (tea) and sang wedding songs.

My wedding day was slowly coming closer. Two weeks before the date, Father had to be admitted into hospital. The feeling of joy and laughter was suddenly gone. Everybody prayed for him to get better. In my mind I had the positive thought that he would be home before the wedding. He was the strongest man on earth. He had to get better. We all depended on him.

A week before the wedding, as was customary among us, the women gathered once again to clean rice, *dholl*, lentils and vegetables to keep in readiness for the cook. Now we were counting the days: Monday, Tuesday, Wednesday – and then came the day I will never forget; that fateful Thursday, three days before my wedding, the message came from the hospital. Father had passed on to the heavenly abode of the Lord Almighty. Suddenly on that sunny Thursday, the light went out of our lives. All activity came to a standstill. The pillar of our lives was gone. The message spread through Rensburgdrift. Everyone came. They lamented his departure. Mother was beside herself with grief.

The next day, Father's body lay in state under the same marquee that was erected in our front yard for my wedding. There was just one question on everyone's mind: 'What about the wedding?' We waited for *Punditji's* advice. After completing the funeral rites with the hymn of peace, *Punditji* informed the mourners that the wedding would take place after the 40-day ceremony. Father was buried in the family graveyard in the corner of the mealie plantation next to the graves of Granny, Grandfather, my uncles and some cousins. 'The soul is never born and it never dies. It is for ever and ever. Weapons cannot hurt the spirit and fire can never burn it. Waters cannot wet it and winds cannot dry it. May we find comfort in these truths, O God.'

Things were not the same after that. Mother wore a white mourning sari. Another date was set for my wedding. Usually the wedding ceremony is the most colourful, elegant and ceremonious ritual practised in the Hindu home. But mine had to be a quiet one, with only close family and neighbours. Then came the weekend of the wedding. The pre-wedding practices were performed. The *Tilak* ceremony, which makes the betrothal official, where the *Punditji* applies the red dot (*tilak*) to the bride's forehead for the first time; and the *Hardee*, where each

57

of the two families contributes some turmeric powder (*hardee*), which is mixed together and combined with mustard oil to make a paste to spread over the bride's body as a cleansing ritual. The yellow of the turmeric is an auspicious colour in Hindu culture. My girl relatives helped with this. These were performed on the Saturday, the day before the wedding.

On Sunday morning everybody was up very early. My sisters helped with my bath and then my make-up. My long, dark tresses were tied in an up-style. Then my mother's cerise-coloured, silk Benares sari was draped over my head. My aunts came into the room. They all oohed and aahed and I burst into tears. I missed my father; I wanted him there on my wedding day. I wanted him to do my *kanya-daan*, the giving away of the bride by her parents. Traditionally, the *kanya-daan* implies that the bride is handed over from her father's care and responsibility to her husband's. I sobbed and so did everyone else. Eventually my sisters led me to the *mundap*, the canopy raised for ceremonial purposes.

 58

Punctually at 10 a.m. my groom arrived with his parents. Our menfolk received them at the gate and the women did the ceremonial welcome. The bride's family offer the groom a sweet mixture of curd, honey and *ghee*, symbolic of the wish that his married life be sweet and that only sweet words should come from his mouth. Then *Punditji* proceeded with the wedding ceremony. Besides *Punditji's* voice, there was silence all around. We took our marriage vows where we promised faithfulness, loyalty, sharing with and caring for each other, which were witnessed by all the guests, and the elders made sure that all the rituals went smoothly and that nothing was omitted. Finally, we took the Seven Steps (*Saptapadi*), each step representing a promise by the new partners for each other's welfare, support, prosperity, long life, and so on.

The *Punditji* asked the guests to rise and shower us with their blessings while he chanted the *mantras* or hymns. Because we were still in mourning, we only had about one hundred guests, but we all shared a wedding feast of vegetarian food such as briyani, pickles, *dholl* and salads. After lunch, it was time for me to leave the home in which I grew up to go to my husband's home to start a new life.

As the car drove out of the gateway, I looked back. There stood Mother, clutching my brothers, and behind her were all my relatives of Rensburgdrift. On that day, a daughter of Rensburgdrift became a daughter-in-law of Pietermaritzburg.

And arranged marriages? Well, I have been married for 27 years now, so it worked for me. I was lucky as I got on well with my mother-in-law and his sisters. We had our highs and lows, but we learnt patience and tolerance, and how to share what we were feeling and make decisions together. I think that has kept our marriage strong. We've tried to teach this to our three children. When I look at the divorce rate in the Indian community today, after two young people have met on the street corner and said they love each other and want to get married, then I think that when the parents intervene there is more stability and they get to know each other and the families better.

Now, many years later, Rensburgdrift is not the same. The elders have passed away and so has Mother. The rest of the people educated themselves and moved to Estcourt and other neighbouring towns. But the houses still stand there. Some are derelict and some are occupied by squatters. The gum trees still stand tall and proud on the driveways, swaying to and fro as if beckoning us to come back.

I go back there sometimes with my family to place flowers on Father's grave and say a prayer for him. Then I just sit and remember all the happy times I spent with him.

59

Boys will be boys – A teacher's story

Shanthee Manjoo

Shanthee Manjoo is a retired teacher who has lived in Pietermaritzburg all her life. She taught at a number of local schools and, later in her career, was the first Indian teacher in Pietermaritzburg to teach at a 'Coloured' school. She earned herself a reputation as an outspoken and unconventional member of various school staffrooms, often questioning authority and championing the children's points of view. She became a well-known figure because of her custom of attending school wearing a sari. This is an extract from her soon to be published autobiography, Classrooms in the Shade.

'*Jai! Jai! Jai! Hanuman gosaai/ Kripa karo gurudev kinhaai …*' His voice rose magnificently from the grapevine that grew at the corner of the garden where he stood singing his praises to the Maker of the Universe, water falling in a silvery ark from the water container in his hand. His voice rose and reached the house of the east where the *moulvi* still lay asleep. And later the call came from the minaret of the mosque: *Allahu Akbar …* God is great! Beads of water gleamed on his shoulder, water from the cold shower which began my father's day, and then, clad in a *dhoti*, he made his way barefoot to the garden where the *jhanda*, the prayer flag with the symbol *Om*, stood. The dew lay on the grass, untouched by the sun. There was a hush in the Maritzburg air. The sparrows hidden in the leafy cover had not taken to flight. The man's approach and his splendid voice had not startled them.

Back in the house Mr Ramkisson, my father, changed quickly into a pair of grey trousers and a neat white shirt, black socks and shoes. Standing all day in front of the huge stove at the Plough Hotel in Longmarket Street, he had no need for a tie. A white apron and tall chef's hat completed his simple attire. He walked every day to the hotel in the White area of the city, and walked back again at two o'clock in the afternoon to rest for an hour or two before returning to work until eight. Sometimes he turned over the rich black soil with a spade, preparing the garden for planting.

 62

Before leaving for work in the morning, my father would enter the large room where I lay on the floor with my sisters, on beds made from long rice bags and sheets with Blue Ribbon Flour printed on them, and a blanket for cover. Years of dedicated service, and still my father could not afford proper bedding for his children. 'Come on, get up, time to get up,' he would call, teaching us the habit of rising early with the sun. We were five sisters sleeping in a row. My mother, a girl bride, had died in her early twenties, seventeen days after the birth of her youngest daughter, when I was only three years old. Our names had been carefully chosen by the Hindi priest who had consulted his books: Dharam Devi, Ghumti Devi (Lela), Shanthee Devi, Gowri and Devika. He lived close by with his family in George Street. Preparing a horoscope for the newly born Hindi child was an auspicious occasion for both parent and priest.

My grandmother Nani often sat on the floor of the room, her right leg drawn up under her. A *bowla* made from a tin gashed with holes and advertising Laurel paraffin would contain glowing coals. It brought warmth to the house in winter, and my sisters and I would creep as close as we dared to spread our hands before the fire. Nani wore white clothes, a symbol of her widowhood. Her silver-white hair fell loosely over her right eye and she was always tucking it behind her ear. She was a tiny figure, yet remained the head of the household, and the entire family loved and respected her.

The infant classes were conducted in the church building of St Paul's in George Street. My father had finally managed to get us into school. I looked down while the teacher squatted before me with a bemused look on his face. 'How many legs has a duck?' he asked again, not unkindly. 'Three,' was my very audible answer. Mr Valentine Nobin leaned closer towards me, 'How many?' This time I did not answer, but the silence was enough. The whole class had heard the answer, and the news spread to the upper class to my sister Lela, and she would not speak to me when we got home, humiliated by her younger sister's stupidity. I hid behind the tall rose trees in the church garden at playtime; the fragrance filled the air and I looked up at the creamy white flowers with their yellow centres. If I could only remain there in the garden, but the bell would ring, jarringly, and I would drag my footsteps back to the classroom. For days I was the butt of the class jokes and I hated school.

Then there was a blustery day with the cold buffeting my thin body. I drew my coat closer. It was a pretty coat. My father had given it to me that very morning and I was happy to be wearing something new to school. My happiness, however, was short-lived. No sooner had the class set eyes upon it than they began shouting, 'Joseph's coat, Joseph's coat,' laughing uproariously. The coat of many colours! My eyes stung with unshed tears. What was wrong with it? I was proud that my coat looked like the one Joseph had worn as a little boy, but I never wore it again, and the wind would blow bitingly, making me hunch my shoulders.

But I have happier memories as well. I remember being wildly excited. My music teacher had chosen me from the whole school to lead the chorus of a song welcoming the girl guides from Baroda. The school assembled in the hall where the visitors from India stood ready with bows and arrows. They were a team of twenty young girls dressed in white shorts and shirts, long black hair neatly plaited. They were about to demonstrate their prowess at shooting targets at the back of the hall. Together with the school, I watched the dazzling performance. The visitors acknowledged the applause by modestly placing their hands together, then going back to their seats. Now it was my turn to sing as I stood before them, my heart racing with joy: 'Star of India, morning bright, shining after stormy night. India's sons where'er they be, ne'er forget their loyalty …' Oh! I was going to that wonderful land with these girls from the state of Gujarat. My father would surely let me go. I would learn, above other things, to speak Hindi faultlessly. Perhaps even see the glorious Taj Mahal by moonlight. That night I lay awake thinking of that land so far away. And I waited impatiently for the night to fade away. Tomorrow I would accompany the girls back to India. My heart sang. When morning came, my father would not hear of it. I cried bitterly, but it was of no use. The girl guides had gone.

•

Sitting in the sun with the headmistress, I was the only student with a Standard 10 matriculation certificate doing a one-year teachers' course, the T3B as it was grandly called. It was the highest course available at the Dartnell Crescent Indian Girls' High School in Durban. My father had found me accommodation with family in Avoca. I had to travel daily on the North Coast train. Of course, there was a Natal Teachers' Training College in Longmarket Street in Maritzburg, in my own home town, but such portals of learning were only open to the Whites, *verboten* to non-Whites like me. Miss Guy was taking me for Organisation of Method. It was very cold in her office, so we had come out for the lesson. The sun was shining down on me. Suddenly I wasn't paying attention any more. I found myself lowering my head towards the ground, feeling faint in the heat. Miss Guy was surprised. 'I thought your pigmentation would have provided for that,' she said. Pigmentation? Up to that moment, this was a new word to me. However, it soon became apparent to Miss Guy that my so-called pigmentation had not helped at all, and so ended my lessons in the sun. My brown skin had failed to protect me from the heat! And so here was I, a young student teacher just out of high school, not in the least bit interested in dark skins or light skins or whether the heat of the sun affected them adversely or not, and here was I having to listen to a word being defined to me, reminding me yet again that I was some sort of an inferior human because of my dark skin. Acutely embarrassed and silenced by Miss Guy's complete lack of sensitivity, I carried my chair back into her office. Hadn't I triumphed, though? I did not have a fair skin and yet I had nearly fainted. I recall now that the incident had brought me nothing but a dull sense of nothingness.

An important aspect of teacher training is the practical work. I was sent to Centenary Road School near Magazine Barracks to deliver an oral lesson to Class 2. It was referred to as a 'crit' lesson, when an experienced teacher or principal sat at the back to listen and critically assess one's teaching ability. My mind was full of ideas for a lesson that would come alive. I rejected the idea of a large picture entitled 'Baby Learns to Walk' as a teaching aid. My cousin had one of the finest flower stalls, just outside the Durban Central Station. When I got off the train that morning, I stopped at his stall and selected a bunch of Californian poppies. The flowers attracted the children immediately. They were an assortment of bright colours. I wanted the class to feel the texture of the petals so I could introduce, among other things, words such as 'silk' and 'Californian poppies'. First, a little girl came up timidly to touch the petals. Another came, and another, to touch and smell. To my consternation, I noticed a bee in the heart of a red poppy. If I looked alarmed or tried to shoo away the bee, my small charges would take fright and the disturbed insect would no doubt claim a victim. So I sent them back quietly to their places and, looking calmer than I actually felt, said to the class, 'We have a tiny visitor here with us. Do any of you know what it is? It's always to be found among flowers.' The children craned their necks and the bee, appearing to sense my predicament, hovered above the flowers and could be seen clearly. 'A bee!' they chorused, more in fun than in fear. My anxious moments were over. Some of the flowers soon looked

65

forlorn, dark petals scattered on the floor. But the class had enjoyed the lesson, the bee's sudden appearance having given them something to talk about. And when I looked around for a vase, a good-looking boy with twinkling eyes and a bright smile ran to produce one from the cupboard.

My best lessons were with Miss Elizabeth Ruth Hunter, a lovely-looking woman who was in charge of the student teacher class. I was her only T3 student; the rest were T5s, which was the Standard 8 certificate. Miss Hunter had a wonderful way with us. I shall always remember the way she taught us to sing the multiplication table so that the little ones could memorise it with ease: 'Two ones are two, two twos are four, two threes are six …' She had a pocketful of ideas.

Another teacher was Miss Enid Hammond, who the girls said always had a favourite matric student. That year it was Fatima Meer, who I can still see in the role of Lady Macbeth, her long hair streaming and with a candle in her hand. I enjoyed every lesson with Miss Hammond whose enthusiasm for speaking and writing good English was unbounded.

66

At the end of the year I had a new friend, Kamala Sham, who travelled from Verulam every day. When the train stopped at Avoca, I got into the same compartment as her and her brother, who taught English at the Sastri College. Kamala took me to a place in Durban, in Grey Street, where the Hindi musical band held their practice. I met the tabla player who became a good friend to me and my sister, Devi.

•

Sex was an unknown word in my youth. Whenever my sisters and I went out to a function, we always sought my father's permission first. He would simply say, 'Behavey yourself', pronouncing the word in his quaint way, but we never laughed, nor did we try to correct him.

Books, I think, gave me an unconscious code of conduct and filled me with thoughts of nobility. From the Richard Halliburton Reader, I became enchanted by the story of King Arthur and the Knights of the Round Table. I dreamed of the Golden Chalice and the Holy Grail. Sir Galahad was my knight in shining armour.

I was in awe of Excalibur and the Lady of the Lake. I sighed with Dante, walking his dog simply to catch a glimpse of the distant Beatrice. Balder the beautiful is dead, is dead! And I marvelled at St George killing the Dragon. I dreamed dreams with the Lady of Shallot, and I pined with Orpheus. The Gorgon's head, alive with snakes, and Pandora's Box, made me tingle with excitement and fear. As I grew older, there were other books and poems, among them *Little Women*, *Forever Amber*, *Beau Geste*, *Lorna Doone* and *War and Peace*. My father brought home *The Natal Witness*, the *National Geographic* magazine, *The Farmer*, and the *British Express*.

At Hindi school Babuji Ramballi Singh, the apple-cheeked *guruji* with silvery hair and gentle humour, provided me with profound thoughts about life in general. He rode to town on his bicycle and he rode back again to his home in Pentrich. He taught me the magic of rich-sounding words in Urdu, the most romantic of the Indian languages, which my sister and I would compare with the simpler Hindi. Babuji also taught me the ballad Draupadi's Lament to God, which I sang at the concert. Queen Draupadi tells of her fate when her husband, the king, loses his entire kingdom in a game of chess, and in a desperate bid to win it back gambles away his dearest possession, the queen herself. Her lament to God is a plea for death rather than submission to her new lord. The *Ramayana*, too, filled me with chaste thoughts. Ravana, the demon king, captured Sita who had accompanied Ram into fourteen years of banishment to the jungle. On her return to Ayodhya, her chastity is questioned; she survives the test and emerges unscathed from the all-consuming fire.

67

Then there were the various beautiful film stars who sacrificed themselves to save others and for a better world. *Sant Tulsidas* was a deeply religious film in which the beautiful woman convinces her husband that seeking God is a far greater quest than his love for her. Along with the many Indian films, there were actors like Charlie Chaplin, Clarke Gable, Errol Flynn, Tyrone Power, Fred Astaire and Ginger Rogers who brought joy into our lives.

A Swedish film on child birth was shown at the Regent cinema to separate audiences over the age of eighteen. The subject did not fill me with curiosity.

After a meeting of the Natal Indian Teachers' Society, I heard someone laughingly ask, 'Can I give you a lift?' It was Mr Naicker, on his motorbike. 'No, thank you,'

I answered coldly. 'You must be afraid of riding on my bike.' That did it. 'I would be happy to ride on your bike,' I said as loftily as I could, 'but not now, I prefer to walk.' He came one afternoon, after school, and we talked of this and that. As he prepared to leave, he pursed his lips. 'You are preposterous, I do not kiss strangers.' He went away laughing, but he still believed I was afraid. So one Sunday morning found me on his motorbike; and, away, with the wind tearing at my hair, and a wild, wild sense of freedom, and, oh, such sheer exhilaration! We sat on a carpet of leaves, turning russet, yellow-brown and gold. He began to talk animatedly. 'Bet nobody's mentioned "penis" to you before,' he said suddenly, thrusting his face challengingly and smiling wickedly at me. I remained silent. The word sounded distinctly out of tune. 'That's funny,' he said at last. 'You should have been giggling by now. Every girl does at this stage.' 'I am not every girl.' His long lashes fluttered with amusement. He threw back his head and laughed and laughed. I saw him again, much later, in Killarney Terrace where my sister Devi was living temporarily. Killarney Terrace was in a beautifully wooded White area. 'I want to ride in that cart!' I said, pointing to a donkey cart driven by a young African boy. 'And so you shall,' laughed Mr Naicker, springing onto the cart and bringing it to a halt with a 'Whoah!' The rhythmic clop-clopping of the donkey cart gave me a great sense of freedom. I never saw Mr Naicker again. They told me he had died. So young, and so full of the joy of living. I could not believe it. Alcohol, they said, had killed him.

•

There had been the persistent Sastri College lecturer whose marriage proposal I had rejected with an outright, 'Most emphatically not!' 'You will marry him,' my father declared flatly. 'No I won't,' I said, defying him for the first time and losing all sense of honour and respect. My father responded by flinging a brass *lota* at me, and I dodged as he chased me round the table. I escaped his wrath by rushing out and, like one possessed, I walked the whole way down Retief Street to Hawthorne Hill where my friend lived. 'I don't care if a car knocks me over,' I muttered, crossing the road recklessly. But that was only a half-hearted wish. I did not want to die.

In 1953 I fell hopelessly in love with the quiet, handsome Muslim, Muhammad Essop Manjoo, whom I promptly named Shyam, an exquisite and celestial name for a beloved. I first saw him in Mr Mayne's senior shorthand class and I simply lived for those Tuesday and Thursday evenings to be with him. Filled with longing one afternoon, I walked to the farthermost upper end of Church Street to I S Cassimjee's where Shyam worked as an accountant. I went disguised as a man, complete with dark glasses and hat, taking my friend Cynthia along for moral support. All for the sweet, forbidden pleasure, excitement and pure joy of seeing and surprising Shyam. Although Aunt, Ma and Mami knew of this friendship, they wisely withheld it from my father who, being a devout Hindu, would never approve. That was putting it mildly! Besides, in his present poor state of health, it would be disastrous to upset him.

My brother-in-law, Harry, however, was my fiercest opponent. I was awakened late one night by Harry's ranting and raving under the mango tree near my window. Mami stormed into the room. 'How is it that you are all sleeping like the dead?' she demanded angrily, 'Can't any of you hear Harry threatening to kill Manjoo?' I always had the profoundest respect for Harry, yet I was the reason why he was now standing under our mango tree, making a desperate bid to bring me to my senses. Oh my God, I had reduced this noble, normally peaceful person to a drunken protester.

But there were other obstacles facing me. I invited Shyam to supper one evening. When my aunt brought the food in, he asked me who had cut the chicken. 'My aunt, I suppose,' I said innocently. 'Then it isn't *halaal*.' 'What of it?' I retorted in a flash. 'It's nicely prepared, and with love, and I should have thought that was all that mattered.' 'You don't understand,' he said gently but firmly. 'But Auntie prepared it for us!' He would not touch the food. At last, with silent anger welling up in me, I flung the plate of food at him, the curry splashing all over his jacket and shirt. It was some time before I could bring myself to dab away furiously at the curry stains. That night I was tormented with doubt. A marriage between a Muslim and a Hindu would never work out.

I decided to consult someone for advice. Mr R B Maharaj, a respected member of the Arya Samaj, lived in Pentrich. He received me graciously. 'I want to get married,' I began unhappily, 'but he's Muslim and refuses to become a

69

Hindu, and I don't want to be a Muslim.' 'Marry him and keep your respective religions.' 'What about children?' I wanted to ask, but felt too embarrassed. 'Go in peace,' he said, placing his palms together, a smile illuminating his handsome Aryan features.

The Hindu community was up in arms about our friendship. The Pietermaritzburg Technical Institute thought it was unthinkable that this young girl had the gall to want to marry a Muslim. 'Shave off her hair, so that will be an example to the entire Hindu community!'

Then there was the boy from a well-known Tamil family in New Hanover. 'Let's make our baby!' he said with an air of smugness, expecting me to fly into his arms. But I was an old-fashioned girl with old-fashioned ideas about the sanctity of marriage, and was deeply offended by the very suggestion. Besides, we were nothing more than friends. His parting shot was, 'Well, now I know the Muslims don't stand a chance!' Walking home one afternoon after I had been to pay my father's electricity bill, I halted as a freshly lit cigarette landed at my feet. 'I had to stop you somehow; I just wanted to tell you that, even if you have a boyfriend, I will still love you.' It was the tiresome fellow again.

 70

Why this deep-seated animosity when Hindus traded with Muslims and played cricket with them? I could not understand. However, at high school I had sensed an undercurrent when the Tamil boys would refer to the Muslims as 'Thoorkas', a term of derision they had coined from the English word 'Turk'.

'Pakistani bitch!' an enraged Tamilian hissed from Moodley's Service Station as I passed by from St Anthony's. 'My, but you can walk fast,' the voice continued as I quickened my pace.

Muslims, like Jews and Catholics, did not marry an outsider unless conversion took place. So, we were married at last, in a mosque in Durban without my father's knowledge. This should have been the happiest day in my life, to share with my father and the rest of my family, and most of all to have his blessing and consent. And here I was being wed in secret, which left me with a profound sense of sadness and disquiet.

Although, in some ways, my father never quite forgave me for marrying outside the Hindu religion, ultimately he became reconciled to my decision and, when the children arrived, he loved them unconditionally and I had no regrets about my decision.

•

In apartheid South Africa it was compulsory for all high school students to learn the second official language, and for typing students to be able to type in Afrikaans. So I asked the 8Cs to bring along their Afrikaans textbooks. Paging through the pictures of *Die Lewende Taal*, I stopped at a familiar picture. It showed the Taj Mahal with the avenue of trees alongside the water. 'Do any of you recognise this picture?' There was no answer. 'Well!' I said in amazement, 'This is a picture of the greatest love story in the world.' 'What! We didn't know,' they exclaimed in unison. 'Please tell us, Miss.' Swallowing my disbelief at their ignorance in matters of universal interest – after all, the Taj Mahal was one of the wonders of the ancient world, I began at once to enlighten them.

71

'There once lived in India a young prince, the Moghul emperor Shah Jahan, who married the beautiful princess Mumtaz Mahal. He loved her so much that, when she died, he felt he had nothing to live for. So he ordered a palace to be built in her memory, a palace of his eternal love for her, something for the world to gaze at forever. When it was finally complete, made of the finest marble and inlaid with precious gems and inscriptions from the *Quran*, Shah Jahan had the princess embalmed and placed in the mausoleum, within the Taj Mahal, which you see here. It is said that seeing the Taj Mahal by moonlight is a never-to-be-forgotten sight.'

'Oh, Miss,' said Melanie, her eyes misty, 'they don't love like that any more.' 'Don't you believe her Miss,' called out Sheila, 'she's been in and out of love a thousand times.' 'That's not true,' cried Melanie, 'nobody's loved me like that.' Melanie was a pretty girl with green eyes and a light complexion and freckles on her nose. 'Tell us more,' said Marlene, 'I want no more to type, the lesson's almost over anyway.' Eager hands released A4 sheets from their typewriters, but there was no cause for concern. I knew that the next day the girls would type the great love story with wonderful enthusiasm. Let them now dream the dreams of some mysterious young prince riding into their lives, bringing the sweet fragrance of love.

•

'Don't teach boys,' they told me, 'you will find it much too difficult. You will end up a nervous wreck.' But I taught at the Haythorne High School for 'Coloured' boys for 14 years, from 1976 to 1990, and only left when I retired from teaching. Boys will be boys, no matter what their colour, and I prefer a lively class to a docile one. You get the nice ones and the naughty ones, the dull ones and the clever ones. I loved my time there.

My first introduction to the boys was when I required someone to paint numbers on the typewriters. There were thirty machines and tables, and numbering them was one way of keeping discipline and strict control. A well-built boy was chosen by the woodwork master to paint the numbers, together with another boy. He was Eugene Anthony Colebourn. I liked him instantly. I was to learn more about him in my English lessons. There was Fabian Carey, who would look at a girl in the way a farmer would size up a horse. 'I've got Irish blood in me,' he said, looking at me with cool grey eyes. 'And I'm of German stock,' said Denver, wrinkling his freckled nose. 'Meet Idi Amin,' said Eugene, drawing a huge fellow to the table. 'Yes,' laughed Martin, 'you've really got to meet him.' The said Idi Amin looked at me and withdrew his gaze. An imposing figure he was, indeed, and ebony black in colour. All of which was probably why his friends had jokingly made the comparison. No mention of a grandmother's heritage. While proudly acknowledging their Nordic blood ties, they had silently denied the cultural richness in the African blood coursing through their veins. I was to discover that pupils in my other classes with Indian blood were just as reluctant to admit their Indian ancestry. Could these youngsters really be blamed for imbibing the apartheid way of life which made them, and indeed all of us, feel ashamed and even guilty of our own roots?

'Yes, Miss, call him Idi Amin.' 'Oh, come on now,' I cajoled, 'I want his real name.' 'Mark,' chorused a number of voices. 'But there's another Mark, Mark Mathey, so you may as well get used to calling him Idi Amin to avoid any confusion.'

 72

'And I,' said Eugene with the faintest hint of a dimple appearing in his cheek, 'am thoroughly English.' 'And I am Russell Hamilton Julius,' said a fair-looking boy, pushing his way through the group, 'and don't you forget that!' I was not to forget Russell in a hurry, or any of the boys, for that matter. All twenty eight of them, with complexions ranging from white, ruddy, brown to black. For in each one of them I was to find something endearing.

•

Then there was Trevor Goss, with his tantalising grin. Whether I was scolding him or busily engaged in teaching a lesson, it did not matter, because he would be watching me keenly and grinning from ear to ear. 'You remind me of the Chesire Cat in *Alice in Wonderland*,' I burst out one day. 'Don't you ever tire of grinning?' 'No, Miss,' he drawled, his grin deepening. 'Wipe that grin off your face at once!' He drew a handkerchief from his pocket and proceeded to wipe his face with exaggerated slowness, grinning all the while. Eugene and Martin rushed out of their places to box his ears, but I sent them back and learned to ignore this irritating behaviour of Trevor's.

The Japtha brothers, Peter and Thomas, who were identical twins, took much pleasure in confusing me with their work. Even their writing was identical. 'Is this your work, Peter?' 'I don't know, Miss.' 'What do you mean, you don't know? Look at it closely.' 'It isn't my work, Miss.' 'Is it Thomas' then?' 'Could be.' 'Stop playing games with me, is this your work or not?' 'It looks like my work, Miss, but I'm not so sure now.' 'How do you expect me to know which is your work, and which is your brother's, when you can't even recognise your own writing? For goodness' sake, write your name on all your written work in future.' 'Yes, Miss, but did you want Peter's work?' 'Well, of course I did; why else do you think we're having this inane conversation?' 'I'm sure I don't know, Miss, but you will have to ask Peter; I'm Thomas.' 'Why on earth didn't you tell me that in the first place?' 'You called me Peter, Miss.'

One afternoon after their woodwork lesson, the entire class gathered round my table and the tall Ivan Dennis handed me a roll of paper. 'We've brought you a calendar for our classroom,' he offered by way of an explanation. The boys drew closer; I was acutely aware of twenty-eight pairs of eyes watching

73

me as I unrolled the paper. A very busty and scantily clad pin-up thrust herself out of the picture to greet me. The blood rushed to my cheeks. The boys stood watching, taking everything in. I looked up at Ivan and Cedric, the boys nearest me, and looked away again. They were smiling at my discomfort. The class stood waiting. 'We … ell,' I managed to stammer at last, 'we did need a calendar, but where were you thinking of putting this up?' I finished lamely. Eager hands grabbed the calendar and placed it in the space right in front, next to the blackboard. 'Oh no!' I protested, 'that will never do! You wouldn't be looking at me at all while I tried to teach you. And I need your attention, not her. I simply can't have that kind of competition. Look at her, and look at me; I just don't stand a chance!' They laughed good naturedly and pinned the calendar at the back of the classroom.

They never gave it another glance. Sometime later I noticed that the calendar had gone. Another teacher, Mr Moody, using the classroom for his Accounting lessons, had no doubt found it objectionable and removed it, but none of the boys questioned its disappearance.

Russell repeated Standard 8 the following year. That year, too, my old typing class increased so that I was no longer teaching English. This was disappointing as I felt I had so much more to contribute by teaching English and watching the class blossom into fine young students of the English language, and developing their keen sense of humour.

As I was sitting marking in my free period, Russell walked into the classroom, head hanging. 'I was sent out of the room just because I asked about "objective writing" for some of my mates, who didn't understand it.' 'Don't you think you should go back and apologise?' 'What, me apologise? I didn't do anything wrong. You used to show us how to write by bringing newspaper reports for us to read.' 'Every teacher has her own method of teaching, Russell. Besides, she's new and young. Just give her a break.' 'What! Are you taking her side already?' 'Shhh!' I said, 'No teacher likes to have her lessons interrupted.' Knowing Russell's penchant for talking a great deal during lessons, I added, 'If you were the teacher and you had a pupil who kept interrupting you, wouldn't you be angry?' 'Now

 74

you're starting on me!' 'Indeed I'm not, just telling you a few home truths. Come on now, what was it that you came to see me about?' 'I have an assignment on poems. Can we discuss some poems?' 'Of course we can.'

Russell left school at the end of the year to join the army. On obtaining leave, the first thing he did was to call at school to see me. He looked so smart in full military uniform. There was an air of confidence about Russell as he spoke to me about life in the army. It was evident that in spite of the strict and rigorous discipline, he enjoyed his new role. The boy had now learned to respect instruction and responsibility like a man. However, my pride in his achievement was tempered by feeling a deep sense of disquiet, considering the brutal role the SADF (South African Defence Force) played in the country throughout the years of apartheid.

Peter is measuring his masculinity with a ruler and Malcolm, seated beside him, shakes his head in silent disbelief. What do I do about Peter? Pretend that I haven't seen him and simply rush along with my English lesson? 'I wonder if any of you have heard of Michelangelo's David?' I begin. 'It is one of the most famous statues in the world, and do you know why? Because he is stark naked! It has been so beautifully carved out of stone that, throughout the world, it is regarded as a work of art. And nobody looks at any special part of his body, giggles and looks away, or feels ashamed, because there is absolutely nothing to be ashamed of in the first place.'

I pause to look pointedly at Peter, who looks back pointedly at me. Does he know what I'm talking about? If he does, then he certainly is not going to let me know. However, I understand that these pupils are at an age when they may not be emotionally ready for the blossoming of their bodies, and there could be a lot of grief in that.

•

He sat there at the corner of Williams Street and looked at me furtively from under his cap. His eyes slid away, but he had to look again and I was smiling at him. 'Morning, Ma'am,' he greeted me, his voice barely audible. He touched his cap diffidently, jumping up at the same time. 'Good morning, Ronnie, enjoying the sunshine?' 'Just sitting, sitting, nowhere to go, no-one to talk to, nobody is interested in me. I sit here the whole day long, and she's the only one who stops to talk to me.' A gust of wind blew some mulberry leaves across. He bent down and, selecting a leaf, offered it to me awkwardly. I took the fragile gift – a bright yellow autumn leaf.

I had been seeing him at the long orderly rows of tables at M L Sultan Technical College. In one of his very first lessons, he sat at the last table in the end row. As I walked round to see if the boys and girls were touch-typing, I noticed his fingernails, bitten to the quick. 'Why, Ronnie, I didn't know you bit your nails.' 'Shhh, Miss,' he said, springing up nervously and trying to hide his hands behind his back. I withdrew his hands gently and placed them palm downwards on the table. 'Please sit down. See, you have nice hands with long fingers, which make it easier to type. Do you think I could look at your hands occasionally? I'd like you to stop biting your nails.' 'Yes, Ma'am.'

 76

That had been a long time ago. Ronnie had left suddenly without completing his year in Standard 8. Had he any friends at all, and why had he not been missed at school? I had had no other contact with him. The family had moved away from Williams Street, and what had happened to Ronnie? Why had he dropped out? What had we as teachers done for pupils like Ronnie, who did not fall in the bright pupil category, who did not do well at school? Did we write them off as no-gooders, sending off reports with cryptic comments such as 'Poor', 'Very weak', 'Does not do well', 'Satisfactory', 'Could do better'? Did we then heave a great sigh of relief when pupils like Ronnie left school of their own free will? But had he left of his own free will? Or had we in some way been responsible for killing all initiative and making life unbearable for some children? Perhaps I had also been one of the causes – teaching in a dull, monotonous tone, or a high-pitched, over-loud voice, or punishing them for the slightest interruption and sending them out of the classroom, or resorting to ridicule?

But now Ronnie was like a ghost of his former self, shrunken and thin, old long before his time. There he sat on the corner of the street, staring into space, seeing nothing and doing nothing, a forlorn and forgotten figure while the world hurried by.

•

For me, looking back, it is a great privilege to have taught children, to have had the responsibility to make or mar their lives. To try to treat them with love and respect, which is so necessary for a relationship with a child; to earn their confidence and trust; to treat each child as an individual; to try to instil in them a love of beauty and of fine language. I have always regarded teaching as a calling, a noble profession. In the classroom I came alive, and somehow it all seemed to come naturally. I loved it!

My marriage

Fazila Gany

Fazila Gany was born in 1963 in Pietermaritzburg, where she has lived all her life. She was educated at Raisethorpe High School and thereafter began training as a nurse but gave it up after a year when she realised that she was unsuited to this profession. She then worked in the Pietermarizburg municipality until her marriage in 1981. After her divorce, Fazila began to work part-time for the project Justice and Women (JAW), which deals mainly with maintenance claims. JAW is based at the Magistrates' Court.

My maternal great-grandfather was originally from India, and all his children lived together in a large extended family. There were five sons who each had their own room, but there was a common dining and living room. What I especially remember is that we children were totally in awe of my great-grandfather because he was the typical patriarchal figure. He was very, very strict with everyone and we were terrified of him. When we came into the house we had to take off our shoes. There were wooden clogs that we had to put on to go outside to the toilet. The house had wooden floors and long passages and we used to tiptoe around so as not to disturb my great-grandfather. We were not allowed to wear the clogs in the house but, when we were little, we would often forget to take them off. We would come into the house with them on and they would go clomp, clomp as we walked. My great-grandfather would yell from his room, 'Who's that?', and we would scurry as fast as possible to remove them. These are some of my earliest memories … I was ten when my great-grandfather died.

 80

My great-granny was a lovely, sweet old lady – very timid. When we went to Durban to visit them, she would sit up at night in the dining room until we arrived. According to my mom she had quite a tough time with my great-grandfather, who was a very difficult man. But the thing that stands out above all was how terrified everybody was of great-grandfather, even his own sons. Whenever he called anyone, they had to go at once and approach him rather like royalty, with their heads bowed and never speak until spoken to. In his patriarchal way, he held the family together. After he passed on, his wish was that his house in Overport be sold. Then everybody got their share and moved on, and the family broke up so that some people didn't see each other very often anymore. My mother had a little earthenware jar that had belonged to my great-gran, which I asked for after my great-gran died, and I treasure that in my house. It's about sixty or seventy years old now.

On my dad's side of the family, things were quite different. We only knew his parents, my grandparents. My granny was the matriarch. She held the power and my grandfather was afraid of her. I still remember her scolding him at the table about his eating habits. She was the businesswoman and held the money, and she was very careful with her money. She ran a flourishing little business selling pickles and samoosas, and my grandfather used to assist her. She had a lovely garden where she used to take us on walks, and we would pick mealies and beans, which we loved.

We lived in the outbuilding of my paternal grandparents' house in Raisthorpe until we moved out to Northdale after my mom had her third child. But my gran was very difficult, for instance when she came to visit us she wouldn't drink from our cups. She insisted on a new cup as she said she would get sores from our cups. But none of my aunts are like her; none of them has that kind of power.

When I was growing up we were quite an anti-social family as we never visited freely. My father only liked visiting if there was a special occasion such as a funeral or wedding, otherwise we never really mixed with other people. Later, when I got married, I found it very strange that my in-laws had visitors every Sunday. It used to drive me nuts because I just wasn't used to it.

After I finished matric I went into nursing at Northdale Hospital which, because I hadn't been exposed to the outside world, I really expected to be Florence Nightingale stuff. But I found that there were a lot of religious issues that caused problems, such as if you were Muslim you were marginalised by the Tamil people. I was very naïve and very committed, and loved what I did, but suddenly I found myself being victimised by a senior sister for some reason I didn't understand. I became very unhappy and decided to leave.

And it was about then that I met my husband and got married. When I fell pregnant with my first child, I left my work for the municipality and became a full-time housewife. My new in-laws were totally different from my family – they had different values, even though they were also Muslims, and even their beliefs were somewhat different. They were far more extreme in their beliefs, whereas my parents had never discussed religion at home. We had been sent to vernacular classes at the *madrassa* but, whatever we picked up from there, we decided for ourselves what we wanted to practise. My parents never imposed any beliefs on us; they just accepted that we were Muslim and we had to pray every day, but the rest was up to us. But it was very different with my in-laws who went to religious

81

functions all the time. Sometimes my husband was so involved with his voluntary religious work that he forgot he had a family. It seemed to me that it was all done to the extreme and I found it all so difficult.

Another thing was that I had been brought up to question things. But when I got married I was like some kind of outcast because I questioned things and did not just accept what my mother-in-law said I should do. My mother-in-law believed that if her mother-in-law did it and she did it, then I must do it. But I was rebellious and said, 'If you can't give me a good enough reason, then forget it, I'm not doing it.' For all the eleven years that I was married, I never lived in my own house – I always lived with my in-laws. My husband was the youngest son and so it was accepted that he would take care of his mom and dad. So from day one I really had it quite rough.

Although my family was not wealthy, we were brought up with a set of values, one of which was that you did not invade each other's privacy. You never went into someone else's room without knocking first, but when I got married my mother-in-law would just walk into my room and open up my wardrobe to pack away my stuff and I used to be so, so angry.

 82

My husband was always mummy's boy. He would listen to me, but always felt I must keep the peace because his mother was the older person. I didn't go out to work – first I had my son and then my daughter, and I began to feel as if I was on loan to my husband's family. When my father-in-law had his bad asthma attacks and the ambulance would come to take him to hospital, I would have to ride in the back with him while my husband went in the car. And I felt more and more, 'What is going on here? Who really cares about me?' There was a constant feeling that I had to bury my true self and live a different life with my in-laws just because I thought I loved a man – their son. But the side of me that questioned and wanted to know lots of things had to be put to sleep, so there was a constant battle inside me. I became highly irritated and frustrated. I had a neighbour who was a friend of mine. My husband disliked her because we spent a lot of time together, and she would say to me, 'How did you ever marry into this family because you're so different from them?' But I kept thinking that there was hope and that things would change.

My husband's whole family would come in for free meals. At first it was quite nice but then it became more taxing because I had to do all the cooking. Even when I was seven months pregnant, they still came. Sometimes about twenty people would rock up, and of course Fazila had to do all the cooking and washing up and cleaning. And nobody helped or cared.

My husband became more and more involved in his work at the mosque. When I woke up in the morning he was gone. Then he would come home for breakfast, push off again to read another prayer in the mosque, come in again for something, head back off to the mosque, and sometimes come back at eight at night with a number of priests for supper. And even if I'd finished supper, I would have to defrost stuff and start to cook all over again. This went on and on and I began to think, 'This is crazy!'

Then I had my third baby. I can't understand why I went on having children when I was so unhappy, but there was always the sense that another child would make him see things differently. If there was a larger family, surely he would see that there's more responsibility.

Another difficulty was that I was never given freedom of access to money. Before I left my job in the municipality, my husband had promised that he would pay for me to study through correspondence and that I could take up whatever I wanted. But, of course, when I did leave, there was never any more talk of that. When I brought it up, he told me there was no money for it. He would allow me to see his salary slip but, when I worked out budgets, he would always make it seem as if we hardly had any money left over. Although he was quite a good mechanic, he never wanted to progress or do anything else himself. I found this very stifling.

It seemed like even my circle of friends was chosen for me – I had to be friends with his friends and their wives. His friends saw me as a threat because I often voiced my opinion, which they didn't like. I know that one friend in particular warned his wife not to be too buddy-buddy with me. She told me about this, but I didn't like this friend anyway, so I didn't really care. Often when I expressed my opinion my husband would slap me and say I was being disrespectful. I was not allowed to say anything that he disagreed with.

83

Eventually I met someone who was selling second-hand clothing. I became involved with this and started getting some money coming in for myself. The problem was that I had to buy the clothes on the credit system and I was getting into trouble. However, I then found a job. An old friend of mine was running an Islamic library and he said, 'We want someone to come in and help. I know you're an avid reader and that you would cope with the job.' Allowing me to go to work at this job was the only good thing that my husband did for me. Of course I had to ask his permission, but he said I could go as long as it didn't become taxing on the family.

My third baby was about two years old at this stage and my marriage was very rocky as I realised more and more how unhappy I was in this relationship. My mother-in-law and I were having numerous fights. Although I believed that one should express one's opinion, I didn't think this meant that one had to go around with one's face pulled up all day, but that was how she would behave. She and I would argue about all sorts of things, silly things like how to feed the domestic worker, and so on. My mother-in-law became quite ill with psoriasis, which kept flaring up, and then she suffered a mild stroke. Although I was now working, I still came home and had to cook and see to the running of the house. When I got married I had decided that my in-laws, who relied on a state pension, would not contribute to the expenses of the household because they were old and should keep their money for themselves. But if my husband made extra money by fixing cars, he would just put it in his pocket and tell me the money was for himself. He would not give me any extra towards expenses.

 84

While I was at work, things went steadily downhill. But I really loved this job and began to meet a lot of different, interesting people. Being exposed to the outside world and talking to people who appeared to be living normal lives made my life seem even more abnormal. Because the job was in an Islamic library, I met mostly Muslim people who came from a variety of walks of life and had different beliefs. I met two young chaps who became good friends. I could sit and discuss things about religion with them, which was very stimulating. But, after about a year, the youngest – Zane – died of an asthma attack at the age of twenty-two. And this was one hell of a tragedy in my life. He had been like a son to me. It was the first time that I had ever lost anyone close to me, and I really felt tremendous loss. I became extremely depressed and was trying to block out all the problems I was experiencing in my marriage.

In the second year of the job, I found out that my mom had cancer. So my marriage was on the rocks, my mother-in-law suffering from a stroke, and my mother with cancer – I felt this was the final straw. I had never been very close to my mother when I was a child, but we had become good friends during my marriage. My friends gave me lots of support at this time. One friend in particular would come in the afternoons and we used to talk and talk before she took me home. I used to sit in the car and say to her, 'I can't bear to go up the stairs to the flat.' And she would say, 'You have to go.' And I would drag my feet up those stairs.

Then I decided on a separation from my husband. I went home to my mother for about six months and couldn't believe that, while I was gone, he went on a minor pilgrimage to Mecca – an *Ummrah*, a lesser *Hajj*. How he had managed to save so much money, I don't know, but he used my contributions as well. He brought me back some sort of a bracelet as a kind of bribe. He didn't even leave any money for the children while he was away. But at the end of the six months, my family and some friends as well as his family put lots of pressure on me to go back. They said things would be different now and he would change for the better. So I went back and found that my husband had done up the flat, which seemed like a little comfort. But the honeymoon lasted for a week and we were back to square one.

We just had nothing in common. When I told him about what I was reading, or the fact that I had written some poetry, he would just not answer or say, 'Oh, that's ridiculous!' We never shared anything and suddenly I just felt that I was married to a complete stranger. I woke up one morning and looked at this man sleeping beside me and I thought, 'Oh God, I don't even love you any more. I could go on if we had some kind of friendship, if you were nice to me; I could go on living with you if we had some kind of understanding. I don't have to love you to

85

live with you, if you were just caring, I could live with you.' And then the thought came strongly, 'Oh God, how do I get out of this?' because divorce is so frowned upon in Islam.

I begged my mother-in-law to just go away for a while to give us some time to try to work this out, and she said, 'This is my house. If you don't like it, you can go away.' So then my husband started sleeping in another room and his mother would make his bed for him in that room. I got more and more desperate because they seemed to be ganging up against me.

Although I had never suspected him of an affair, I had felt that he was having an affair with the religious institutions. In the Muslim community, having affairs is highly frowned upon, but I had never had the excuse to complain that my husband was unfaithful. When I told my friends about how bad my marriage was, they would immediately ask if that was the problem. But then I found that my husband, who many thought was a saint in lots of ways, was trying to make up to the girlfriend of my brother-in-law's friend. My sister had found her hysterically saying that my husband was making passes at her, and wanted to go out with her. Suddenly I thought, 'I wonder how long this kind of thing has being going on? The wife is always the last to hear about these things.' So I thought, 'At last I have something to torture him with.'

I didn't tell him directly that I knew, but I started passing little hints and he suddenly realised that I knew something. But instead of becoming nice to me, he became more and more terrible to me. We eventually stopped communicating altogether, which was dreadful for me because I can't live with someone and not ever talk to him. We lived like this for about eight months, with the only communication being notes stuck up on the mirror. There had always been a lot of violence with him just striking out at me for no apparent reason. But I had been brought up with my mother saying, 'You never lift your hands up to your husband, you never hit him. It's just quite unacceptable to do that.' But I now decided I wasn't going to take any more hidings. I started throwing things. I broke some lovely crystal vases throwing them at him, and even broke a window. A short time back he had assaulted me and I had gone to a doctor who knew us both. The doctor

 86

said, 'If he does this again, you come to me and I'll fill out those forms and get an interdict. You tell him that I'll personally sort it out.' I had bruises on my eyelids and elsewhere. And then I started getting migraines, and would go home and take a pill and wash it down with cough mixture, which would give me a nice drowsy feeling that totally blocked out my surroundings. Once I got into that, I began to do it more and more often. I started having all my meals in my bedroom so I didn't have to watch him and his mother eating, with their atrocious table manners.

Then we had another huge fight. Every time this happened, the children would run crying to the neighbours. So I called my father and told him what had happened, and said, 'I can't take any more, and I want to come home.' And my father, being the Muslim patriarch that he is, said, 'You just stay there and sort out your problems. This is your marriage, you fight it and you sort it out.' He just didn't know how to deal with it and couldn't take the responsibility, although he always acted like a powerful person at home. Of course, he also wanted to save face in the community because of the terrible stigma that Muslims put on divorce and he didn't want to have a divorced daughter. My response was to go and find my mother-in-law's tablets for high blood pressure. I took a whole handful and swallowed them. My father-in-law had come into the bathroom and grabbed me and put his finger down my throat. But my husband said, 'Let her die!' It was then I finally decided that, whatever happened, I was out of that place. But I didn't leave just then.

The doctor put me on some tablets for depression, but I still couldn't see how to get out. I knew nothing about the law and didn't know what to do or where to turn. I had a lot of friends in the flats where we lived because I was friendly to everyone, and often baked and sent them things. They were well aware of what was going on in our household. One of the old men downstairs had said to my father, 'You'd better take your daughter away from there,' but my father couldn't listen.

Then one evening I just went into my mother-in-law's bedroom and started pulling armfuls of her clothes out of her wardrobe and shouting, 'I want you out of here, both of you!' Of course, my husband was paying the rent so it was pretty crazy, but I just had to have room to think. I had to have space to sort something out. Something snapped in me; all hell broke loose, and all the years of abuse came

87

to a head. I got violent and started throwing things, throwing their clothes out of the door. Everybody was screaming hysterically, and the neighbours came out to see what was going on. Then I went to the kitchen drawer and got out a very big knife, and I said, 'If you don't move out now, I will kill all of you.' They were terrified and scuttled outside, realising that I had totally lost it. They were calling to the neighbours and saying, 'Do you see what she's doing?' I locked the gate and shouted, 'Don't one of you try to come in here or you'll see what I'll do!' I'm pretty sure that if they had tried to approach me, I would have popped them – I had reached such a stage. I understand how women kill their husbands after years and years of abuse and oppression. All that suppressed anger comes out. One of the neighbours came to speak to me and I fell on the floor sobbing. She said, 'You can't stay here any more,' and she called the doctor who came and sedated me. He said to me, 'What the hell are you still doing in this marriage? You should have left a long time ago.' Then they took me away from there, to my sister, because I couldn't go to my father.

 88

One needs to understand this whole issue of divorce in the Muslim community. For me it was never worrying about what the community thought. I'm just not the kind of person to worry about that – I really don't give a fig about what the community thinks. For me it was an issue between me and my Creator, between me and God. We were brought up with the idea contained in an Arabic word, *Arsh* (the throne of God), that when somebody gets divorced, the throne of God actually shakes because he is so unhappy at the break-up. God wants families to be happy and marriage is something very sacred. And I kept thinking, 'Am I going to anger God in this way; do I have sufficient justification to do this?' But because of my fairly extensive reading in Muslim literature, I knew that God didn't want me to be in this miserable kind of situation, where there was no communication with my partner and the children were being damaged. But I had to be sure that I was making the right decision and that I wasn't going to turn back. On that day when all hell broke loose, however, I no longer cared. I just wanted out, but I knew somewhere inside me that it was the right thing to do, that God wasn't going to be angry, and for me that was hugely important. I wanted to be sure that I was religiously correct and that I wasn't going to incur God's wrath. Now, when I think about it, this was very silly because I needed to think about the forgiveness of God. I should never have stayed the whole eleven years in that marriage.

The whole process involved the issue of being a Muslim woman. I lost my sense of individuality. I had never been exposed to real life and I have learnt so much from this experience. I know that if I had to live my life again, I would have to do exactly the same and get divorced again. I will never let go of the peace of mind that I have achieved now. Through all the struggles of being a single parent, the financial issues and everything, I have never missed marriage. I have achieved my independence, my own individual self, and can now help other people. Some people still find it strange and, even after eight years of being divorced, they still say to me, 'Don't you wish you could get back together with your ex-husband?' I just look at them and think, 'Are you absolutely crazy?' Because I remember having nightmares about being back with my husband. The feeling was too terrible, and when I woke I thought, 'Oh God, thank goodness it's only a dream.'

It's really strange how many Indian families want to push all their dirt under the carpet, never wanting it exposed because it's just not acceptable to expose these things. If it's not supposed to happen, then you pretend that it's not happening. Suddenly my ex-husband was exposed. Of course, if a woman walks out on her marriage, she has to take the rap. She is seen as the rotten one. I was the one who had given up and he didn't need to take any responsibility. He's never forgiven me and would be very happy to see me destroyed, and every now and again he tries to get back at me. So, although I'm divorced, I'm really not free because he has a hold over me through my children. He knows where my weaknesses are and how I care about the children's sense of security and well-being, so he uses them to get to me. He tries to make them see how wrong he thinks I am, which upsets them and me as well. So, I often wonder, 'How free and divorced am I really?' I understand now that it is better to be a widow in this Muslim community because, when you are a widow, there's finality – but divorce does not bring finality. You are somehow still attached to that man.

89

In some ways, then, I have rather isolated myself from the community, perhaps because in my work for Justice and Women I see so many awful things that happen to women. When I get home I don't want to have to deal with any more problems. And I am tired of answering questions like, 'How are you, really? You've put on weight.' I know they're thinking, 'Are you very happy that you've put on weight, or is it because you're not happy?' I just say, 'It's the single life and I'm very happy, thank you.' Sometimes I just ignore them because I'm tired of it all. The Muslim community is so small in Maritzburg. Everybody knows everybody, and you wonder what they're thinking. Some of my previous friends are no longer so friendly because their husbands have given them ultimatums: 'You can't be friends with this woman because she's wild; she left her husband.'

 90

I'm also worried that my son, who I love so much, is growing up with many of the beliefs and values of my ex-husband. This really feels at times as if it's destroying me. As a feminist mother, there is this clash of religion and culture. My son was really exposed to a lot of the violence. I remember when he was ten he saw me kneeling on my prayer mat and crying, and he said to me, 'You know, Mum, if it's so bad, let's go.' And I think he carries quite a lot of guilt in him. Perhaps he thinks if he hadn't said that then I would have stayed in the marriage. But he's growing up in lots of ways to be like his father, and I try so hard to get him to look at things broadly, but he finds it difficult. He goes to the same mosque as his dad and I'm scared he is being brainwashed.

I hope that my two daughters are able to see that I've become a very strong woman, and how I've survived. As Indian women, I don't want them to feel that they've got to live up to other people's expectations – to be good, obedient women; to be obedient, submissive wives; even to live in *purdah*; not to speak what's on their minds, but to stifle their own opinions. It's all very difficult and sad what it means to be an Indian woman. The real test will be when my children get married – what kind of a mother-in-law will I be? Who am I, really? I just know that I'm proud to be an Indian woman, even if so much is confusing and changing.

A tribute to my jailer

Nina Hassim

Nina Hassim was born in 1936 in Cape Town. She studied for a BSc degree at the University of Cape Town where she was a founder member of the Cape Peninsular Students' Union (CPSU). After graduating, she joined the Society of Young South Africa (SOYA). In 1961 she became a founder member of the African People's Democratic Union of Southern Africa (APDUSA). All these organisations existed within the Unity Movement. Nina came to Pietermaritzburg in 1963 where she continued to work for APDUSA, frequently being picked up by the police for handing out pamphlets. She completed a pharmacy degree at the University of Durban Westville and then worked as a pharmacist in Maritzburg, supporting her family while her husband, Kader, was detained and later sentenced to eight years of imprisonment on Robben Island. In this story she describes part of her experience in 1971 when the Security Police held her in detention, in solitary confinement, for 78 days under Section 6 of the Terrorism Act in order to try to persuade her to give them evidence that would incriminate her husband who had recently been arrested. This story was published in The Natal Witness *in August 1998 during the Truth and Reconciliation Commission hearings as part of 'The Way We Were' series.*

There are many stories of the bond that develops between jailer and jailed. This tribute does not describe such an incident, but is a story of courage and kindness and the great humanity of one man and his family in the dark days of repression and the Terrorism Act.

As the Truth and Reconciliation Commission comes to an end and the horror of the past lies naked to the world, it rekindles some of the memories of the people who lived through those terrible times. Now it is time for me to take stock and record a painful period in my own life for those who remain. It will show that courage and humanity were not entirely absent, and not all agents of the state were savages. To those who resist attempts to force them to forgive, this is a reminder that it was possible to make choices. Perpetrators of violence did have choices. They chose violence. The alternative took courage.

94

Remembrance is saddest every year on that day in autumn when the chill wind off the Drakensberg presages the coming of winter. The remembrance is most acute then, and the pain almost physical. In the autumn of 1971 I was a detainee at the Hilton Police Station. A habit that lives with me to this day is that I stubbornly refuse to add the extra blanket that will give me a better night's sleep. It is as if the delay is a test of will. In the morning the station commander greeted me and asked if I had slept. When I replied in the negative, he suggested that I might have been cold and that he would give me extra blankets. I replied that I did not think so, but he later insisted on giving me the blankets and I reluctantly used them that night. And I slept – what bliss.

Every year I resist the blanket and every year the memory of those days returns. This has nothing to do with the events of the detention and everything to do with my inability to set out the way Mr Rust treated me. There, it is out at last. Dick Rust – the name I feared I could never pay proper tribute to without in some way hurting him or his family.

Dick Rust is gone – but never forgotten – and, in the only way I know will assuage my deep sense of gratitude for having passed through his life, I wish to record for those close to him and to me and for anyone who cares to know, a story of courage and humanity.

The first time I set eyes on Mr Rust I was in the hands of the Security Police who had earlier that day detained me under the Terrorism Act. He was supervising (for want of a better word) the hosing down of the cell in which I was going to be placed. He was the station commander of the Hilton Police Station.

In solitary confinement one of the most difficult things is the loneliness of being hours and hours with oneself and one's thoughts and fantasies. Each day Mr Rust opened my cell and greeted me and brought me hot water to wash, as there was only cold water in the shower. Each night he came to lock me up and once again greeted me. Whenever I was alone and not with the Security Police, the cell door was left open and I could go out into the small courtyard which was adjacent to the cell. The door of the courtyard was kept locked, but I had the freedom to move between cell and courtyard where there was a shower, basin and toilet, and I could take some exercise. This was a great kindness which I believe was almost unique compared with other detainees.

But that is but a small part of what he did. I cannot remember details of all the things that happened, for many years have passed, but the most important events are still clear. It is these that I try to describe.

On the second day of my detention, after I had been interrogated through the day and the night, in the morning there was a knock on the door of the interrogation room which clearly caused some consternation. One of the security policemen opened the door and I heard a voice ask, 'Mag sy kos kry?' (May she have food?) There stood Mr Rust in the doorway with a tray of breakfast. Obviously irritated, the security policeman allowed him in to place the tray on the table. I was then allowed to eat. It was the first time for hours that I had been allowed to sit down. The breakfast tray was beautifully laid out with a white cloth, and I believe that both his entrance and the way the tray was laid out were to bring me closer to a better world, away from what had been happening over the previous hours.

In that brief moment, I realised that he was not someone to be afraid of but someone I could trust. In the weeks that followed, his greetings in the morning and at night helped me to keep my grip on reality and prevent me from sinking into a stupor. It was not the food or the Ovaltine, obviously purchased to help me to sleep through the tension about whether I was to be released or not – being discussed as part of a 'deal' between lawyers and the Security Police, and dependent upon the whim of the latter.

When the day finally came that I was told I was to be released, I was hesitant to step out of the safety of Mr Rust's custody because who knew what sinister tricks the Security Police had dreamt up? I only packed and left when he confirmed that indeed I was being released and that he himself had seen the release order. His whole expression exuded joy that he was able to confirm my release and be there to witness it for he had looked after me for 78 days.

These things were a small part of what he did for me, the true extent of which I only learnt later.

I also wish to pay tribute to Mr Rust's wife, Jo Rust. Deep down I knew that there must be a woman who made the trays of food and placed something special on them to tempt me to eat. I had never seen her, but I had heard a lovely voice and glimpsed through the keyhole the outline of a woman who occasionally passed through the police station yard. One night, in the midst of a fierce electrical storm and heavy rain, I heard a voice calling my name. That was the day I was supposed to have been released but had not been. Mr Rust had been deeply troubled by this and informed me that no one would explain what was happening when he phoned the Security Police. In retrospect, his even daring to phone them was remarkable.

The voice I heard was that of Mrs Rust, although at the time I did not know her name. She spoke to me through the barred windows and this beautiful voice expressed such anguish that I had not been released, and such love and care and compassion for a fellow human being, that I shall never forget that night. Her thoughts for my family and especially my children touched my soul. Her words of encouragement and deep sense of pain eased my own pain and fear.

After I was eventually released and was able to visit them later, I remember my heart beating through my rib cage. All the while I was driving there I was watching in case I was being followed, and so would bring trouble to these brave people. I remember the beautiful china and tea and cake they had prepared for our first meeting as equals – no longer prisoner and guard.

As we spoke they made it clear to me that I had nothing to fear on their behalf as they had broken no law or regulation in their dealings with me when I was a detainee, and that they had nothing to be afraid of. How little they knew of the lack of respect the Security Police had for law or regulations. Perhaps they knew only too well but valued their own moral code far higher than fear of the Security Police. They then felt free to tell me the real way in which they had protected me. At no time could the Security Police have had unrestricted access to me because two keys were needed to obtain access to the cell in which I was kept, and one was kept at all times with Mr Rust.

The horrors of the apartheid security machine have slowly become known. We may never know the whole truth. Against this background, the story of the Rusts stands out as an example of the nobility of spirit that comes to the fore when principled people are faced with moral dilemmas in times of upheaval, war and catastrophe. Mr Rust had to apply unjust and reprehensible laws – the mere mention of the Terrorism Act in those days instilled real terror, but his conduct was exemplary. His behaviour to me showed compassion and he used regulations as far as was possible to protect and shield me. As an ex-soldier he treated me in the way a prisoner of war should be treated.

This story took a long time to be told: at last it is done – undiminished by time. I salute you, dear commandant.

The Mughal Tapestry Project

Shano Suparsad

Shano Suparsad was born in 1945 in Pietermaritzburg. She is the youngest sister of Vidya Satgoor and so, like her, grew up in the largely Hindi-speaking community of Plessislaer. She went to school at Sutherlands Primary School and Indian Girls' High, and then trained as a teacher for one year at Springfield Training College in Durban. For three or four years she taught at various schools in and around Pietermaritzburg, but her lust for travel then took her to India where her sister, Githa, was training to be a doctor. During her eighteen months in India she worked in an informal school for rural children who had accompanied their parents to the city. After her return home, she worked in trade unions for a while before becoming involved in library work in poor communities. She currently works in a library in Pietermaritzburg. Shano speaks Hindi fluently and has recently started attending Sanskrit classes.

When the phone rang one morning in March 1996, I was surprised to hear the voice of Kobus Moolman, the Education Officer at the Tatham Art Gallery. He wanted to ask me whether I could help to get a group of Indian women together who might be interested in becoming involved in the Mughal Tapestry Project. He knew that I had contacts with a lot of women in Northdale as I had been doing library work there for some years. I was very interested and my two sisters, Vidya and Githa, were immediately enthusiastic, and so the group began to form.

At the beginning of 1996, the Natal Museum and the Tatham Art Gallery were invited to become involved in this international textile project that had been organised by the Victoria & Albert Museum in London. This remarkable and exciting project resulted in drawing together a group of local Indian women from a cross-section of Tamil, Gujarati, Hindi, Muslim and Christian sections of the community.

It all started when Linda Ireland from the Natal Museum met Shireen Akbar at the Victoria & Albert Museum. Shireen explained the details of the project which she had devised, and suggested that Indian women in Pietermaritzburg might like to participate. The Mughal Tent Project planned for a brilliant red tent to be erected in the garden of the museum, which was to be decorated with brightly coloured textile panels designed and hand-made by groups of women and girls from the British South Asian community. It was planned as part of the Victoria & Albert Museum's celebrations of the fiftieth anniversary of the independence of India and Pakistan in 1947. The museum's South Asian Educational Initiative wanted to encourage South Asian British women to explore their cultural heritage by introducing them to the vibrant and exciting collection of Indian treasures housed in the museum, to assist them to appreciate their own rich tradition and so be inspired to create art works of their own. For many it was their first opportunity to access the wealth of material in a museum collection. Here they were able, for the first time, to come face to face with aspects of their history, culture and religion which – until now – they had only heard or read about. The choice of the Mughal and Rajput tent idea was stimulated by those depicted in the miniature paintings in the gallery. These tents were to symbolise the romance of the nomadic life and to suggest the insecure lifestyle of migrants and refugees experienced by many diaspora Indian families. For these women the tent was to be a powerful symbol of their link with the past.

Each group of women was given a piece of red fabric, ten feet by four feet, in the shape of the *mihrab*, the niche that faces towards Mecca in a mosque. On it they were to use techniques such as embroidery, painting and printing to create a panel that expressed something of their personal experiences and heritage.

Finally, when the exhibition was opened on 26 June 1997, over fifty richly decorated panels – made not only by women in Britain, but also from India, Bangladesh, Pakistan, the United Arab Emirates, the USA and Pietermaritzburg, South Africa – were displayed in rotation in the purpose-made tent. Over 800 women from nine different countries had participated in the project. As the largest project ever tackled by the education department of the Victoria & Albert Museum, it had taken six years to put together.

101

In Pietermaritzburg we started our part of the project with twelve women whom we had contacted by word of mouth. We began to meet every Wednesday evening at the Northdale Technical College. As we talked and talked, we became very excited by the idea that at last there was some interest being shown in Indian culture by the formerly all-White museums of Maritzburg, and that we might be able to put the Indian presence in the city on the map. We also soon realised that it would be necessary for us to explore the whole question of our identity, both historically and in the present, to discover a new sense of ourselves as Indian women and South Africans. We needed to look at our ancestry, our religious traditions, and our culture in a more detailed way than most of us had ever done before. Who were our ancestors, where had they come from, where had they settled in South Africa, and how had they suffered and struggled with apartheid? We discovered that almost all of us had been affected by the group areas removals, which helped bring a strong sense of solidarity. Here we were, a group of middle-class urban women, becoming extremely excited at being encouraged to explore our backgrounds and to discover and understand new aspects of ourselves and our lives.

With the help of the people from the art gallery and the museum, a number of workshops were organised to help us do this, and to encourage us to discover what artistic gifts we might have since most of us were very intimidated by the thought of producing art. None of us thought we could draw, let alone paint, but we were about to discover differently.

At one of the first workshops, to get things off the ground, we were asked to bring some object with which we felt a strong personal connection, and which expressed an important aspect of ourselves. Some of the things that were brought included somebody's grandmother's wedding dress, a beautiful colourful sari, an oil lamp, some statues of deities and other figures, and various photos, and these got us talking about family treasures and what people value.

We made a couple of visits to various museums to view collections of Indian art, such as a beautiful statue of the Hindu god Ganesha, all sorts of brass artefacts, a model of the Taj Mahal, paintings, tapestries, and so on.

 102

As the weeks passed we gained new members until we were about thirty women who formed a really interesting variety of the community in Maritzburg: housewives, a doctor, teachers, businesswomen, a scientist, and a couple of artists. In general we worked well together, although at first some people were shy of members from other communities. At times we argued about what was important to include in our panel, and some women tried to push their own interests, so we disagreed quite heatedly with one another but also learnt how to compromise so that no-one felt left out.

Later we started to meet at Brenda's house in Mountain Rise because many people were afraid to go into town at night. Brenda had a big room, which she converted into a workroom, and we used to have tea and cake every time. The reason we all kept coming was because we were really enjoying it so much.

The workshop in which we learnt about Madubhani painting was one of the best and most helpful. This is a traditional, ritualistic craft from the village of Madhubani in Bihar, north India, which is mostly done by women. It involves painting personal and religious symbols on the walls and floors of houses for certain ceremonies, such as weddings and funerals. Many of the women in our group had ancestors who had come from Bihar, so they had some identification with the area. Elmarie Nel, a local art teacher, showed us how to do this on papier-mâché plates. We found this very exciting as we realised we were reviving a traditional Indian technique and adapting it for our own purposes here in our project. But, what was most exciting and got everyone highly enthusiastic, was being helped to explore our own ideas and creativity and finding that we could make something attractive. By the end of the session, each person had made a plate using Indian motifs and colours. Gradually people were beginning to feel confident about their artistic ability, which was very empowering.

We also had sessions on wool dyeing, the symbolism of colour, appliqué with mirrors, and basic design. We learnt a wealth of new techniques that we had never thought existed. My sister Githa was delighted to discover just how gifted she was at embroidery. We were having great fun, but for many weeks just couldn't work out how to put all these ideas together, what to put in and what to leave out. Would we ever be able to produce the expected panel?

Finally we decided that we wanted to depict something of our whole history in South Africa, with all its hardships, pains, achievements and joys. And how people had adapted to their new lives in a strange land and reached where we are today.

At the bottom of the panel we decided to start with the ship, the *SS Truro*, in which the first indentured labourers came to South Africa, with mirror work to depict their tears at the sadness of leaving their motherland. The design moves upwards, showing the lives of the early settlers first working in the cane fields and, after completing their indentures, branching into market gardening with a woman carrying a basket on her head, and a trading store, a reminder of successful commercial ventures. A colourfully decorated Indian pot symbolises the many festivals and weddings celebrated. Another pot has African designs with the word *ubuntu* embroidered close by, showing the meeting and melding of the two cultures in KwaZulu-Natal. A school is held under a tree, a reminder of the fact that no school buildings existed in the early years, and a book and musical instruments emphasise the importance of education and the arts in our lives. The political hardships suffered during the apartheid era, especially the

103

forced removals, have been recorded in a tombstone with the words 'Rest in Peace Cleland, Pentrich, Edendale, Plessislaer', reminders of the pain incurred when Indian communities were moved out of these areas. A spinning wheel represents the Gandhian period in South Africa, and Maritzburg in particular, with Ghandi's seminal teachings of *ahimsa* and *satyagraha* (non-violence and truth force/passive resistance), stemming from his eviction from a train at Maritzburg station. At the top of the panel the various religions of the Indian settlers are given pride of place to emphasise their importance in our lives, both in the past and the present, with a temple, a mosque, a church, and a Buddhist stupa. And the very top has a flame emerging from a lotus flower, symbolising the search for light and truth at the heart of all religions.

In June 1997, four of us – I, my sister Githa, Hemla Makan and Brenda Vather – who had all been enthusiastically involved in the project for so many months, left for London to represent the team at the opening of the exhibition. London was amazing. As we walked through the grand entrance to the Victoria & Albert museum on a wet cold day, it was like a dream come true. It was truly magnificent and all so beautiful – the great tent in the garden with thousands of Indian people from all over England and elsewhere. It was so exciting and we suddenly realised that we were not inferior nobodies from South Africa, but part of a global community. It gave us a sense of pride such as we had never experienced before. Here we were, and we had produced something beautiful and worthwhile which other people from all over the world were admiring.

The Victoria & Albert Museum treated us so warmly and gave us each a pass so that we could go back there as often as we liked. I went back every day for the whole week that we were in London. The Indian collection there was the most wonderful thing I had ever set eyes on. I had never seen such beautiful stuff in my whole life – the paintings, the tapestries, the jewellery – and I just couldn't get enough of it. To think that all this is part of our rich Indian heritage – what a tremendous sense of pride to recognise we belong to this!

Eventually our panel came back from England. It has been included in the newly assembled permanent Indian exhibit in the Natal Museum, which was inspired by the Mughal Project. And so we achieved our desire to put Indian history and culture into the museums of Maritzburg.

In various ways the project has changed the lives of those of us who participated. The revival of traditional Indian arts and crafts, and the close working together of women from different religious and cultural backgrounds for so many months, created this tremendous sense of warmth and pride in sharing a vibrant and ancient heritage. Many women came from very closed and conservative families and communities, where they had not met other women outside their circle. Suddenly there was a great opening up, a breaking of barriers among different religious groups and a realisation that we are all one. This rare opportunity to reflect on our roots and our vision of ourselves has greatly reinforced our self-esteem and identity, both as Indian women and as post-apartheid South Africans.

Githa felt very strongly that we shouldn't let the enthusiasm and interest die, and that we should form an ongoing craft group, but she died of a heart attack before this could happen. However, we have formed the Truro Quilters who meet on the first Tuesday morning of every month. Four of the original Mughal Project women are involved, and I take the day off in order to be able to attend. We are taught by Marlene Turner of Maritzburg, and have produced some great stuff. So the creativity goes on, and perhaps some day we'll produce another tapestry which will hang in the city hall.

105

Why I became an activist

Naseema Aboo

Naseema Aboo was born in 1950 in Vryburg in the northern Cape, where her parents, the Ghoors, were in business running Ghoors Department Store. She went to an Afrikaans school named 'Colinda' because it served the Coloured and Indian communities in the town. Naseema was one of two pupils in her matric class. Later she studied a BA degree in Education and Islamic Studies through the University of South Africa (UNISA). She and her husband moved to Pietermaritzburg in 1989 where she became highly involved in the Women's Islamic Movement which does a wide variety of social work.

We are just ordinary people, but this is not the image that the media portrays of us. We formed the Pietermaritzburg Islamic Action Group to protest against the war in Afghanistan, and to try to help make some sense of world events after the September 11 bombings of the World Trade Centre. We were all shocked and horrified at what happened. It definitely does not represent what Islam is all about. We care for the lives that were lost then in America, and we also care about the lives being lost now in Afghanistan. When this group was formed, we women said to the men: 'Whatever you do, don't exclude the women. We find that at rallies and meetings there is a good response from women, and women are losing their husbands and children in the war, so women feel for other women.' So women are playing an active part on the committee. While we are outraged at what is happening in Afghanistan, we also need to fight poverty and injustice in our own country.

We want to help counter the misinformation that is being pumped out by the United States (US). When we question this information, we are called callous and told we do not care about the more than five thousand people who died. Of course we care. Our *jihad* is not to go out and fight, but to gather accurate information and pass it on, to help people to understand what is happening. We want people to look at what is happening, to think about it logically, and to engage with the material.

It is important to let people know that Islam is not about violence. We have a strong message of peace but, as so often happens, and it happened again after the two peace rallies we held in Durban, the media seems determined to misrepresent us.

Two rallies were held in 2001 in Durban, shortly before the outbreak of war in Afghanistan. The first was in the Durban City Hall, and three bus loads of people went from Maritzburg. The hall was absolutely packed. We all felt highly charged up by the feeling of solidarity, but I also experienced a feeling of helplessness about how little we can do to change the course of world events. Fatima Meer was one of a number of fiery anti-war speakers. After the speeches we held a candlelight vigil outside. The whole crowd started chanting 'Allahu Akbar' ('God is great') as we began to move round the building. Suddenly I saw a man lift his son onto his shoulders and the child was brandishing a toy gun. I quickly went up to him and said, 'Please, no gun. We don't want that.' But he simply ignored me – and that was exactly what one newspaper chose to highlight in illustrating the evening's activities. Little was said about the speeches at the rally, or that people from different religious groups were speaking from the platform. We have a strict code of conduct that we all dress in regular clothes, with no Pagad-style masked faces or guns or burning flags.

At the next rally in Durban in November 2001, we held a march from the beach front right up Smith Street to the American Consulate, where we intended to deliver a memorandum and petition to the Consul. We followed Muslim protocol with the women in the front, then the men, and family groups at the back. But the Consul was not there, so some of the men became angry and called for him to appear. It was then that the SABC (South African Broadcasting Corporation) cameramen suggested that they burn the US flag they were carrying, which was done. The situation became very volatile until one of the priests stood up on the steps and started praying in an attempt to pacify the crowd. It was amazing – suddenly everyone joined in. But, of course, the images of the flag burning were what went out to the country.

In every religion there are extremists and ultra-conservatives, but these are mainly minority groups. Most Muslims really do not want to see war. Part of our campaign is to educate Muslims about the media's promotion and encouragement of the 'Muslim terrorist' stereotype. Muslims are under constant siege all over the world and we don't want our children to grow up in a world that hates Muslims.

Despite being part of a patriarchal culture, the Indian woman is the force behind the household. The Muslim woman is actually very strong but is seldom recognised. Even during the apartheid era, Muslim women played a very strong role but were often not recognised because religious issues always held them back. You couldn't be in the forefront when it came to marches; you couldn't be in the forefront when it came to voicing your opinion; but many women were well educated and realised quite clearly what was happening in the country. A lot of young women were encouraged by their mothers to go and protest; if it hadn't been for the mothers, they wouldn't have gone out there. With the *Quran* behind

109

us as our constitution, we had the motivation to fight the oppressor. We were performing a religious duty as well as a social duty: to fight being oppressed. It wasn't easy in those days because the minute you said something against the regime, you were likely to be locked up. And many women were locked up, like Fatima Meer who fought tirelessly and is still fighting, even from her sick bed. And they were our role models and we should follow in their footsteps and know that women can do it.

So, I'm very grateful to my parents, especially my dad, as he taught us what to do, how to go forward fearlessly. He believed education for girls was very important, and if you educate a woman you educate a nation because the children grow up in the laps of their mothers. If the woman is educated, then the children are educated. As I reflect on growing up in South Africa during apartheid, I realise, ironically, that we gained a lot. Growing up in our group areas, we kept our culture intact; we kept our religious schools and all they taught us about our culture and religion. Although we objected to being confined to that area, we gained strength to fight against the oppressive government. And, in the seventies when they tried to move us out of our homes, we fought against them.

 110

My mum, too, was very strong. She came from India in 1948, when she was only nineteen years old, to join my dad and get married to him. She got off the ship at Lorenço Marques in Mozambique and took a train to Johannesburg, where she got married to my dad, and then they took a train to Vryburg. What a hell of a distance to go! She simply had to adjust to her new life and learnt to speak fluent Afrikaans and communicated with all the locals. She is a wonderful woman.

We had a good life in Vryburg where I grew up. We had a good relationship with the Coloured community and with the Whites. In the business there, running the store, we interacted with a great number of people which influenced my attitudes. My father believed in throwing us in at the deep end and would often ask us to help look after the business and to take over in various departments. It all helped us to grow up to be responsible. It also supplemented the very limited education we were getting at the little Afrikaans school there. My father's mother also helped in the shop after her husband died. She persuaded my father not to sell cigarettes in the shop because she objected to smoking. She said people buy them on 'tick', smoke them up, and then forget to pay for them. So she said, 'All cigarettes out of the shop!' and we never saw cigarettes in our home. She was a strong force in my dad's life.

We sometimes got into trouble with the police because we were not supposed to invite White or Black people into our homes, but we did. My very good friend was a Jewish girl who later went to Cape Town University. When she came home for the holidays and came into the shop to see me, I would run and hug her, and my father would say, 'Careful, you mustn't hug White people in the shop. You'll get into trouble.' I couldn't accept that I had done anything wrong. It was all so stupid!

I was still very young when I became aware that there was discrimination against people of other groups and a lack of respect for them. In my father's store, if people spent a large amount of money, he used to give them a gift. A farming couple bought a lounge suite from him so he gave the two children a gift each. The father said to the little boy, 'Sê dankie vir die geskenkie' ('Say thank you for the gift'), and the child said brightly to my father, 'Dankie, Oom Coolie.' The parents were very angry with the child for embarrassing them so. On another occasion a man praised my dad by saying, 'You are good, like a Christian; you treat everyone so well, just like a Christian.' And my father responded by saying, 'I'm not a Christian, I'm a Muslim; see, here's the *Quran* and here's the Bible, they come from the same source.'

I learnt that when there's a struggle in life, you have to fight to achieve what you want. But when life becomes easy as it has now, we lose that zeal to fight; the struggle is over now and the new dispensation is making everybody sit back. Young people of all colours in this country have become complacent because things are too easy.

In 1974 our whole family was forced to move away from Vryburg when our properties were expropriated. We went to Brits in the Transvaal because there was an already demarcated area for Indians and we didn't want to have to move again. My father put up a very big building there for another shop, which he called Hagels. Once again my sister and I helped my dad to run this department store.

111

After I got married in 1977, I moved to Laudium, a suburb of Pretoria, to live with my husband who was in business as an accountant in Johannesburg. We preferred living in Laudium because it was much more developed and more comfortable than Lenasia in Jo'burg. We stayed there for eleven years and had four children in that time, and then we went to Maritzburg in order to run my husband's shoe factory, which was being mismanaged.

And maybe it was God's will to bring me to Maritzburg because the children were now all at school and I could go back to complete my degree. I also got involved with community work through the Women's Islamic Movement where we worked with women's groups and children's groups, and then with the upliftment of the Black community. In this movement, money is raised by the women for women's projects. We make the decisions on how to spend the money for ourselves. We get support from the Sufi Mosque in East Street, the only mosque in Maritzburg where women are allowed to worship.

 112

The first project that we tackled in the Black community was the McCarthy 'tent school'. There had been a farm school on the McCarthy's farm but, when it was sold, the school was forced off the farm. So they all went to the police station to say they had no school. The police got hold of a lot of army tents for them to use as classrooms, as well as a lot of desks. Then I was phoned by A S Chetty of the city council to ask if I could do something about organising some food for the 300 children. I got together a group of women to help and we found they would need 45 loaves of bread a day, five days a week. So the Women's Islamic Movement contacted the Hindu Women's Association and the Sai Group to help with organising the food. We formed a small committee and got the bread to them every day, all put together in sandwiches. The next thing to do was to try to get them a proper school building because the children really couldn't be left in the tents, especially in the rainy season. We had to do a lot of persuading to get a meeting with the town council and to get the Department of Education involved.

We battled for three years before we managed to get the United Nations involved in funding and were able to have a simple corrugated iron school built. So we went from a tent school to a tin school, which became known as the Azalea Primary School, with the attendance rising to 550 pupils. We continued to feed them and the attendance rate was 89 per cent because of this. But unfortunately, when we could no longer go on taking the bread to them every day because we had many other projects, and we tried to persuade them to come and fetch it from us, they refused, so the feeding stopped. We felt very disappointed, but we believed it was time for them to take some responsibility for their own project.

In Sweetwaters we have arranged for the children at a school to come by Kombi taxi every day to fetch the food that we have organised for them, which is working very well. Once a year we do a blanket distribution to this and other communities, such as the Ash Road informal settlement.

A recent initiative is our seedling project, where we distribute vegetable seedlings to certain communities with the aim that we all start greening our back gardens and growing as much food as possible to help sustain our families. And this can help to empower the women. God has given us the land and we should make good use of it. We have lost the culture of growing things and we need to recover it.

113

We have a very big problem with regard to women in our community. Ideally the Islamic religion does not oppress women, but the Indian culture does. So the men tend to do what suits them best and follow what is accepted in Indian culture. Women in the lower economic group suffer the most because they have little education and are economically dependent on the men, so they become victims of abuse.

I belonged to this group called Sanzaf. It stands for the South African National Zakaah Fund, which was formed in the early seventies. *Zakaah* is the Muslim charitable giving of two and a half per cent of one's excess wealth or income – that which is left after all living expenses have been catered for. It teaches people to share and to help those less fortunate, to try to uplift the poor. It's a way of 'cleansing wealth'. So Sanzaf is there to organise the distribution of money that individuals donate to the fund from their income. Through bursaries we have been able to help a number of deserving people to gain a good education, and the organisation has assisted many abused women. There is an office where they are able to come for help, and they are given a monthly hamper of food. On Tuesday there are classes for them on religion and social values, and on Thursday big pots of food are cooked for all those who come in for a meal. At religious festivals there is a celebration and all the adults and children who come are given a little gift. Many women have attended from many different backgrounds – Tamil, Hindu, Muslim and Christian.

For example, one of the women we became involved with was married to a man who drank too much. Now in Islam you are not supposed to drink, so he was ashamed of the fact that he was breaking a rule of his religion. This led to him abusing his wife, both emotionally and physically. She told us that when he got drunk and aggressive, he would hit her and she would often hide behind the TV. But one night, when he was very drunk, he smashed the TV. She was terrified because he was in such a rage that she feared he would hit her badly, but the only place she could think of to go was behind the TV. He was so drunk that he just sat in his chair looking at the TV, not noticing that it was her face he was seeing. Finally he fell asleep and she was able to move away. This woman was in dire straits, but she managed to raise all her children. We gave her as much help and support as we could until her husband eventually died. Now her children are able to help support her.

 114

Then this White woman came to us for help. She had converted to Islam because she had encountered Muslims in the Cape and thought Islam was a lovely religion. She came to KwaZulu-Natal where she met and married a Muslim man from Pietermaritzburg who had divorced his wife and was looking for another relationship. He was widely known as a con man who owed money. A number of people warned her against him, but he convinced her he had a lot of money and promised her all sorts of things. It wasn't long before the relationship became unpleasant. He became hooked into watching pornography on the Internet all night, which shocked her as she didn't think this should be part of Muslim culture. They had a child, which she thought might improve the situation, but of course it did not. We told her that the man had a terrible reputation around town and the best thing to do would be to leave him, which eventually she did. But she had no job and said she couldn't support herself and the child, so she was threatened with destitution. We agreed to support her financially for three months by paying her rent and buying the groceries, after which she would have to take responsibility for herself. She was very grateful and agreed that she would look for work. The husband kept threatening her and her little boy, and we did our best to support her. However, when the three months had passed, she said she couldn't get a job so we would have to continue our support. When we pointed out that we could not offer indefinite support, she was very upset and quite angry with us, saying we would have to look after her. It all became very difficult but has finally been resolved after many months as she has left town in order to get away from the husband who was still pestering her. Sadly she has given up Islam and returned to the Christian faith.

Unfortunately the executive committee of Sanzaf is usually all men. It is the women who run the offices, but the men make the decisions. When I first came to Maritzburg, I got myself onto the executive committee which had its meetings in the morning with a curtain between the men and the women. I became very unpopular when I started questioning why certain resolutions had not been carried out, and it was decided to change the time of the meeting to seven o' clock in the morning, an impossible time for me. As long as you are a 'ja broer' ('yes man') to the men it is okay, but they feel threatened if you speak your mind.

Also, increasingly, I have a problem with this kind of charity because I believe that the system we run there, instead of empowering people, tends to make them more and more dependent, which degrades them. They become so dependent on the food and hampers that they don't bother to move on and try to help themselves. They remain there for the rest of their lives and begin to feel that it is their right to be continually supported by others. Even when the initial problem has passed and the children are grown up, they still keep coming and seem to want the dependency – they know nothing else and we are not helping them to find something better. There's something wrong somewhere with all this charity. We are not really uplifting people, which is our aim. We need to help women to gain some kind of training so they can find jobs. They need to be able to become more financially independent.

115

It's a very frustrating thing to do, this charity work. Poverty is not something that is easy to deal with. It is a terrible thing. I always say that the worst thing God can do is to put you in a situation where you are poor and cannot help yourself. That's when women get abused. Even when a man comes to give you a grocery hamper and sees your helpless position, he is likely to say that he'll only bring you another hamper next month if you allow him to enjoy certain privileges. What can a woman do? And this is what's happening, even within the religion. So none of us are safe after all.

Islam is a beautiful religion – it lays down the social norms for all believers. If you look at the impact that Mohammad, a humble man of peace, had on the society of his day – on moral issues, on social and women's issues, on how one should be a husband and a father, he's one of the greatest leaders the world has ever known. He left a legacy for us to follow. But I think all Muslims are going through this problem where their culture and religion are all mixed up. They think this is Islam – and this causes the difficulties, especially for women. Islam does not oppress women.

 116

In the end I'm very grateful to Islam and to my father and my husband, the two men in my life who have helped me to become what I am today. I know that I grew up rather differently from many other people, and that was good because it made me very strong too. My husband has never tried to hold me back in all the work I've done and all the committees on which I've served. When there's a trusting relationship, then one can do a lot of things. My father, too, was very encouraging and gave us a great example of doing charity work. From the *Quran* he believed it was our responsibility to serve humanity, which has had a powerful effect on me. I have tried to pass this on to my children as well because I believe it is very important. All we can take with us from this world when we die is the good deeds we have done. Whatever religion you are from – Muslim, Christian or Hindu – you are going to have to account for what you have done. It doesn't matter what religion or colour you are. In the end your duty is to do what you can to serve humanity and, in doing so, to serve God.

Into the forbidden city

Nalini Naidoo

Nalini Naidoo was born in Pietermaritzburg in 1956 and educated at the Indian Girls' High School. She completed a course in journalism at Rhodes University and took her first job in 1978 on a Community Development Project in the Ciskei, helping people affected by the forced removals to become re-established. She worked as a journalist on The Natal Witness *and left for a while to work part-time at the Natal Society Library. Nalini enjoyed this so much that she did a Higher Diploma in Library Science at the University of Natal before returning to* The Natal Witness. *This story of childhood memories in apartheid-era Pietermaritzburg was first published in* The Natal Witness *in June 2000 as part of the 'Tales of the City' series.*

We only ever made four or five trips and our route was always the same. From Berg Street where we lived, through the Forbidden City, past the graveyard and to our final destination – the Secret Steps.

There were usually five of us, sometimes six. The cousins, my older brother, and me. Weeks were spent planning. There was the way through the city to be plotted, money to be saved for supplies, and meetings to prepare for the dangers ahead. Most importantly, our stories of where we were going had to be co-ordinated. We were certain that if our parents knew how far from home we had strayed, we would be in for a good walloping.

Our first stop was Sutton's Tearoom at the corner of Berg and Boshoff Streets – long since closed – for supplies: thick meaty slices of polony and crusty white bread. From there we walked straight up Berg Street and into the Forbidden City. We walked quietly, my cousin Sally – the toughest and bravest – our self-appointed leader. My brother, second in command. Our leaders had explained why we weren't supposed to be there, something about a Group Areas Act. They said the residents would chase us or, worse still, the police could pick us up.

 120

So we spoke in whispers and trod softly, explorers in a foreign territory, stealing furtive glances at the strange inhabitants – the man mowing his lawn, the family sitting on their verandah enjoying Maritzburg's warm sunshine. We smiled at each other when we saw children just like us playing in their gardens and quickly diverted our eyes when any of them looked our way.

It was exhausting keeping silent so we soon weaved our way back through the little lanes that dotted the Forbidden City to common territory – Commercial Road, where our leaders told us Black people could walk freely. Here we could laugh out loud, skip and chatter about the rest of our adventure.

Next stop: City Tearoom for cream buns, cooldrinks and sweets – Zulu mottos, nutties and pinkies. We sucked our sweets as we walked along, trying to hide our nervousness from each other as we faced the most frightening part of our journey – the walk past the graveyard.

The dangers here had been spelt out at all our meetings. How the spirits could stretch their ghostly forms over the high green hedge and pluck us up to be lost in the underworld forever. We walked at the edge of the kerb in single file with our arms linked and did not make a sound lest they hear us.

It was no use crossing over the road because the cemetery was on both sides. But this was part of venturing into new worlds, so we soldiered on over a stretch that seemed to last forever. Once over this dangerous hurdle we were within reach of our final destination – the Secret Steps.

By this stage all the scary stuff had made us hungry so we hurried to have our lunch, usually under a willow tree on the banks of the Umsinduzi River that flowed at the bottom of the steps. Chunks of bread and polony were washed down with Crerar's cola champagne, Maritzburg's own cooldrink and our favourite because it turned our mouths bright red.

The rest of the afternoon was spent exploring the steps, which seemed to go on forever. What we found fascinating was that each level introduced a new landscape of flowers, shrubs and trees in bright and mottled colours. Leaves and pods in strange shapes and sizes and, of course, a range of insects – butterflies, lizards and beetles. When we grew tired of looking at nature, we would go back to our favourite pastime – watching the White owners of the Secret Steps and its hidden gardens. I remember once saying that they seemed to be such happy people and our leader remarked: 'Why wouldn't they be when they own so much beauty?'

Once or twice we were lucky to find a wedding party having their photographs taken in one of the gardens. We'd keep out of sight behind the rockery and watch these beautiful people in flowing robes, all silks and laces, adding to the fairytale magic of the place.

Over the years I had completely forgotten about these childhood forays. It was letters from our cousins who had emigrated from South Africa that brought back memories of growing up in Maritzburg. I sensed a nostalgic tone in those letters that asked about the Forbidden City and the Secret Steps which made me ponder the concept of 'home' – perhaps it is where your childhood memories are made, no matter what the circumstances. Yet remembering those adventures also reminded me of how, as children, we never felt we belonged in Maritzburg. We were always the outsiders – visitors in our own city.

Today, Maritzburg feels like home and I can recall my childhood with a sense of amusement. I often catch myself smiling as I drive through the area above Boshoff Street, past the Commercial Road cemetery or the rockery in Alexandra Park. And in writing to my cousins and a host of friends who have long since left, I feel a growing intimacy with the place I can now call home.

'Dear Sal, yesterday I drove through the Forbidden City. Remember that house with the big fig trees in the front garden? A Black family lives there now.'

Who am I?

Roshen Latiff

Roshen Latiff was born in Pietersburg in 1960 and educated at the Pietersburg Indian and Coloured School up to matric. She then went to the M L Sultan Technical College in Durban to train as a teacher, but didn't complete her studies as she met her husband-to-be, Omar, there and soon got married. The young married couple spent about a year in Newcastle, her husband's home town, before settling in Pietermaritzburg where Omar had been appointed as a lecturer at the university. Since then Roshen has started studying a degree through UNISA.

I was talking to one of the other mums at a parents' meeting at St John's where my two daughters are at school. Suddenly she said to me, 'It must be so difficult for you because you've pulled your daughter out of an Islamic school and put her into a Christian environment, and then when you go back home you've got to cook lovely food for your husband and you are not allowed to sit down at the table and eat with him.' 'Oh really,' I said, flabbergasted, 'you being an educator, don't you know that we are living in South Africa and we are both mums living in first world conditions? And I live in an equal marriage.' 'Oh! There must be very few equal marriages,' she said weakly, as though she didn't believe me. It was a real shock to me that she couldn't believe there can be equality in a Muslim marriage. There she was, having met me at numerous school meetings, and she had felt this great pity for me and the need to save me from an awful situation. This was an eye-opener for me; I had no idea how ignorant so many people are. When I told my friend Sally, she laughed and said, 'I could see for a long time that she was trying to save you, trying to educate you to Western ways, and that you are supposed to sit at the table with your husband.'

 126

Some time later, a very close friend of mine, Jane, came back from the States and invited me for coffee. We've known each other for many years and have much in common. We went to the Mugg & Bean coffee shop, where she had asked three other friends to join us. Before I could even get my coffee to my lips, one of the women said to me, 'So, you're one of Jane's friends and you're Muslim, right?' 'Yes,' I answered, 'I'm Muslim.' And this started it all over again. They just bombarded me with one question after another, questions like: What are you doing to educate your children not to become terrorists? Why are the Muslims so angry that such violent behaviour is provoked? Why don't they do such crimes in their own countries, instead of going to the States and other Western places? I asked them whether there were no Christian terrorists, and they just looked at me. I wanted a nice social tea to talk to Jane, and this was what I had to deal with! I can't answer those kinds of questions, nor do I want to. I know that it's fear and ignorance on their part, but I had to say, 'I feel the same way as you all do about violence and terrorist activity. I'm very sorry but I can't answer your questions, and I'd just like to enjoy my coffee.'

So this is what I'm dealing with all the time. I understand that these other people are apprehensive about all sorts of things in the world, but so am I! It all seems such crass insensitivity. It is really tough being a modern Muslim woman.

Even in my book club, where we meet once a month, one of the women asked me, 'If Islam is a religion of peace, then why is the Muslim world involved in so much violence?' And this is the type of question I've got to keep trying to answer for people who I think should know better.

It's amazing the misconceptions that people have about others in different communities. Apartheid did its job well; it kept us apart and ignorant. Yet now we're supposed to be learning about each other, but some people don't seem to want to move. And that woman at the parents' meeting is teaching at a high school!

All this hurts me very much. I've heard too that when there are children's birthday parties, some mums say it's easier not to invite the Muslim kids as there are too many problems and restrictions. And some kids said to my daughters, 'You're too brown to come to our party.' When I heard this, I said 'What restrictions are you talking about?' They said, 'Oh, of course you know; the *halaal* thing, and so on.' And I said, 'Don't you even have a cheese roll in your house?' So then the woman said, 'And you're not allowed to touch dogs.' I had to ask, 'Who says so?'

My personal battle is with this stereotyping of Muslims, which happens in the media and then is believed and spread. There is such fear and disdain for us! What I want to do is to get women to come to my house and to say let's talk about these things. We need to come to understand and trust each other. Let's open up to each other.

Part of the problem for us Muslim women is that there is a tradition we want to retain, which is what we grapple with. I don't want to be a slave to tradition or to Western ideas and values, but the need just to be, to be real, is so difficult. When I step out, I perceive things that are so painful, so confusing. I want to retain most of my religion without being utterly conformist and ritualistic, but I'm also a modern woman and don't want to be stereotyped. That's a real burden that I have to bear. I don't always eat curry, much as I love it; my children – and we all – absolutely love pasta! When I was in England recently, many people we met just couldn't believe that we were from South Africa. They couldn't place our accents, and they said to us, 'We hope you enjoy your stay here and have a safe journey back to Pakistan.' 'No,' I kept saying, 'not Pakistan, South Africa.' So it does happen in other places too.

There's also the great diversity of Indian culture in South Africa. Newcastle was my first exposure to this because, in Pietersburg where I grew up, we lived in a very conservative, rather closed, predominantly Muslim community. Most people were in business. I was lucky, however, because there was a high school there so I was able to complete my matric which many girls at the time were unable to do.

 128

Getting married very young opened opportunities to move around that I would not otherwise have had, but it's a kind of Catch 22 because who says marriage is easy? Moving to Maritzburg was a whole new kind of experience because I had always had family and friends to fall back on, and now we had to organise a flat to live in and all sorts of things. It was all very different and it took me nearly two years to settle in. Then there was a shortage of teachers and, because I had already done Nederlands and Psychology through UNISA, I went to teach at Woodlands High School. This was yet another culture shock with the variety of different Indian groups, getting to know the surnames, and becoming accustomed to the different language groups and different foods eaten by those of different backgrounds. But I developed new friendships in this way.

I continually encounter this difficulty in being a Muslim woman because somehow the perception of a Muslim woman has changed. For me it is that much more difficult because I am not a typical Muslim woman, I am a modern Muslim woman. So it's complicated, and that is my battle. I have continuous debates with myself and others about this. In the Muslim community, I'm often considered not to be portraying a proper image there; then I get into the Western groups where I have some dear friends and where I feel I belong, but even some of them don't understand my attachment to my Muslim culture. Sometimes I feel as if I am going dilly because I know I am Muslim and I know that I'm Indian, but I often just don't know exactly where I fit. Do I really fit in or belong anywhere? There's always this push and pull of who I really am, and this often brings a lot of guilt. Why am I not conforming to what is expected of me, why am I always asking questions, and why can't I just be a regular Muslim housewife? But I constantly question. I can't just accept all the old traditions, especially since I have had a lot of political exposure and have met many people from all sorts of walks of life, and also live with Omar and meet his highly intelligent, questioning friends.

During the years when Omar was mayor of Maritzburg, I met some fantastic people, but there were also others who were not. I was on my own at home a lot as he often had to be away at official functions, although I had to be available on demand to attend various functions as well. We never removed our telephone number from the directory, so we got quite a lot of abusive calls. Often I was alone at home and so had to take these calls. Some of these I found deeply unsettling and I became very aware of how insensitive people can be. One night when Omar was out and the children were asleep, an Afrikaans woman phoned and was very abusive. It was *Diwali* festival time and she went on a rave about Indian people trying to run this town. I was shocked and tried to speak to her reasonably, but my daughter heard and woke up and started crying as she knew something was wrong. So the woman said, 'I don't care if your child is crying, my dog is sick because of you Indian people and your fireworks; you're destroying this place and you'd better tell that husband of yours to come and sort my dog out.' And I just had to put the phone down because she wouldn't listen to anything, but she phoned again at six the next morning and started all over again. It was another instance of stereotyping and lumping all Indians together. I knew that some of what she was saying was a reality, but I wasn't part of it and it wasn't my fault, and she wouldn't allow me to speak or explain.

I've blocked out a lot of the anger and hurt because I learnt so much during that time, about people and different personalities and how they react. And there were some marvellous people. The best of all was when I met President Mandela – such an amazing person. I was seated next to him at a lunch when he visited Maritzburg. I had ordered vegetarian food so as not to have to worry about *halaal*, and his food came before mine. He refused to start eating before I received my food, even though we had serious time constraints and had to move on quite

129

quickly to the next part of his itinerary. I begged him to start eating, but he said, 'I will not go ahead; I will eat with you.' And I was so touched at his gentle consideration that, if there hadn't been a whole table full of people, I would have burst into tears. Such absolute dignity! I was so lucky to be a participant in that meeting, which was another and different experience of how people can behave with sensitivity and respect for one another.

I truly believe that we can all get along with each other, and that we can respect one another's religion and pray together at times. My daughters go to chapel at St John's, but some mothers say, 'Why are you Muslims going to chapel, a Christian place of worship?' I am sometimes so afraid that my children might become anti-White, and that must never happen. I am happy for them to attend chapel and have that experience and learn about Christianity in that way. Perhaps then they won't be as ignorant as some of the so-called Christians I have met and, for that matter, as some of my Muslim friends! We all need to broaden our horizons as much as possible.

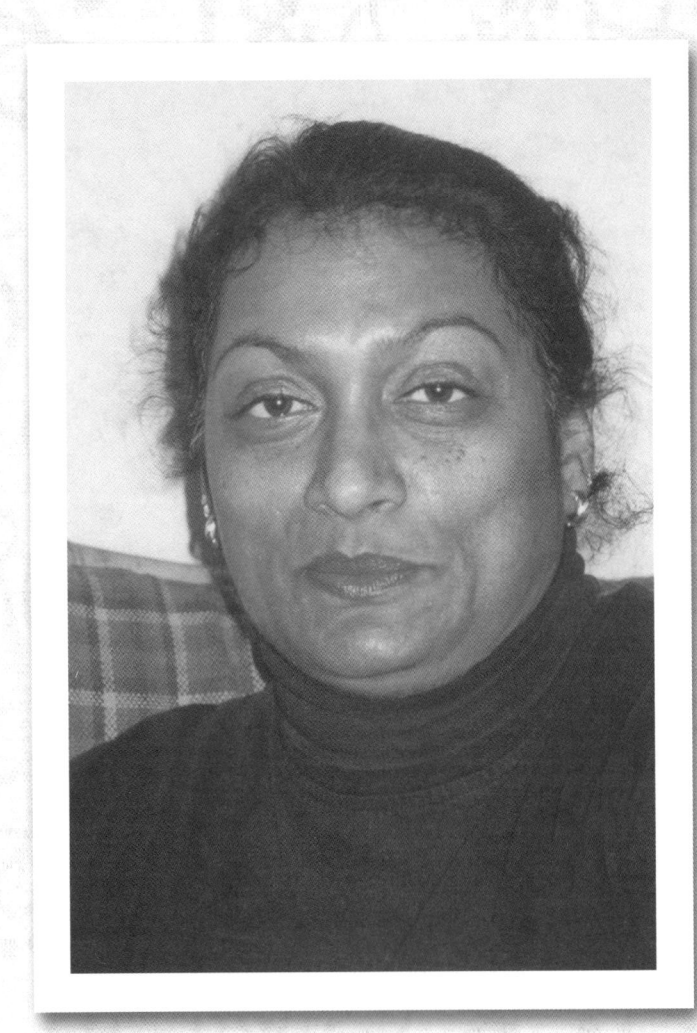

Two marriages

Saras Moodley

Saras Moodley (not her real name) was born in Pietermaritzburg in 1961, and was brought up and educated in Durban. She attended the S M Jhavary Primary School in Clare Estate and the Rise Cliff High School in Arena Park. Soon after completing her matric, she got married. In the early 1990s she trained by correspondence to be a teacher of children with learning disabilities, and at present she teaches at a high school in Pietermaritzburg.

When I was sixteen and in my matric year at school, I was invited to the wedding of a relative of one of my mum's friends. She said my mum should bring me along as she would love me to meet the groom's brother. Being only sixteen, I was very flattered by this and of course agreed to go. I put on my best sari, a lovely blue hipster number that revealed my midriff. When I met the boy, Prem, I immediately noticed how good looking and charming he was, even though he was ten years older than me. I thoroughly enjoyed the wedding and was invited to go to the house after the ceremony, which I was very pleased to do, but quickly changed into a little black dress with spaghetti straps and a pointed handkerchief hem. I thought it was appropriate to wear something more Western to this part of the celebrations. Although I was very shy and naive, I spent most of the evening chatting to Prem and had a really good time. I do remember, however, that when he saw me in the black dress he said, 'If I have anything to do with you, you'll never wear a revealing sari like that again.' I just smiled. At the end of the evening he made a date with me. When I asked my mum if I could go out with him, she said 'Fine'. So, for the rest of my matric year I went out with him which I found very exciting and flattering. Luckily I got through my matric, turned seventeen and left school.

 134

About six months later we decided to get married. We went to a registry office, although we planned to have a traditional Indian ceremony later as we both thought that was the only way to do it properly. My parents were quite happy with the marriage as we were both from Telugu backgrounds, the same religion, and they thought he had good prospects. My father-in-law was so happy about it that he couldn't wait to rush off and buy me a beautiful red silk Benares sari for the traditional ceremony. It did occur to me that I would like to have been allowed to choose my own sari for my wedding, but I thought I should be grateful to him.

The traditional ceremony, which we had in January 1980, was very elaborate and it all seemed so romantic to me. First there was an engagement ceremony where lots of friends and family came over to the house and brought trays of sweetmeats, as well as my sari and jewellery. On the day before the wedding there is a cleansing ceremony, which is great fun because all your women cousins come round to help. They help you rub turmeric powder mixed with water all over your face, arms, legs and body, which is believed to be very cleansing and to give your skin a beautiful glow. Some of the women get naughty and cheeky and try to put their hands up your legs while they are applying the turmeric, and everyone laughs loudly and happily. Then you have a bath to wash that off, and come back for another ritual of putting various types of powder over your body. Then you put on a pretty sari for the rest of the evening.

The next day is the wedding with the special sari, all the jewellery, and the beautiful hair that is only done to Tamil and Telugu brides. Your hair has to be long and plaited, and then yellow and red carnations are plaited into it, which spread all the way down with little bells at the bottom. It is absolutely exquisite. On top of the sari is a lovely gold belt round your waist. Then there is the *mala* necklace, which is made up of 24-carat gold sovereigns. Both the bride and the groom wear one on their wedding day. If your family doesn't have one which is passed down, then you hire one.

The traditional ceremony is very ancient and beautiful, with lots of ritual. There is a *pacha pandal,* a sacred area where you take off your shoes, which is brightly decorated with fresh greenery such as banana leaves and marigolds. I had about a thousand guests who were fed vegetarian food, which is traditional, five or six curries with rice, and many pickles and salad, and we ate off banana leaves. We made our vows in Sanskrit, which of course I don't understand, but we were very serious about it and I thought it was all for keeps, never imagining that it would end up the way it did. It is tradition to wear a *thali,* a yellow string round your neck as a sign of your marriage commitment.

Thinking back, I believe the reason I was so keen to get married so young was that I came from quite a dysfunctional family, where my parents just weren't on the same wavelength, didn't see eye to eye at all, and had little in common. So I think I was really keen to get away from home and start doing my own thing.

Later that year I had my first child, a girl, which I found exciting. I had a good pregnancy and the birth was a terrific event in my life. I settled into married life very happily. I loved doing housework like cleaning, washing and cooking, and then

135

waiting for my husband to come home. At weekends we visited parents in Durban. My husband was involved in the export business and was doing extremely well. He was an ambitious, clever man, but very easily bored.

We had another daughter the following year, and I began to find Prem more and more domineering. His way was the only way, and he would argue for it even when he knew it was wrong. I wasn't really allowed to have any opinions, or to speak much in company, and he would often put me down when I said something, or rudely cut across my conversation. He often talked down to me, as though I was stupid and not as intelligent as he, so I felt quite often that I was still this sixteen-year-old girl, just supposed to be nice and entertaining, just a pretty face to take around and nothing more. But I was starting to grow up, so I argued with him. We also started arguing about how the children should be treated. He usually let them do anything they felt like, even if it was very annoying or even dangerous, and I felt they had to have some discipline. Often he would let the children eat chocolate just before supper, and then they wouldn't eat their food and I would be annoyed. I believed we should agree with each other about how to bring up the children. He shouted loudly when things didn't go his way. Then Prem's business began to suffer badly from the sanctions against South Africa. Having two children now and financial problems, which went from bad to worse, became very traumatic for us.

 136

We had been good friends with my cousin, Ravi, and his wife, and saw a lot of them. But then his wife became very ill and eventually died, leaving him with a young baby son. Prem and I were really both extremely naive and, when we realised we couldn't keep our home, we suggested to Ravi that we should move into his house as it would help us financially and be a comfort and support for him. I needed a secure place to take the children because I was afraid we would lose everything, even the house we were busy building at the time.

At first all seemed to go well and the children played happily together. But Prem spent less and less time with us so that Ravi, the children and I did more and more together, going out and enjoying ourselves. I suppose we were both in a bad place at that time, but when Ravi let me know that he had always been keen on me and fancied me since I was a teenager, I suddenly found myself falling very deeply in love with him. He afforded me this space to be my own person, whereas I had been experiencing such highly dominating behaviour from Prem. So now, with Ravi, things were very different and I was allowed to voice my own opinion, do things my way, and it was all such a relief.

Amazingly, my husband even encouraged Ravi and me to take the children and go off to the Wild Coast for the weekend, where we had a wonderful time. Why he did this I'll never understand, but maybe he was just so taken up with trying to get his finances sorted out that he had no idea of what was going on. Really, he was too busy to care. When we got back and were talking about the weekend, my daughter said something about Uncle Ravi kissing Mummy. And Prem said, 'Pack your things, we're moving out.' My response was, 'No, I'm not going. Where do you think you can take me to? You can go.' So he went.

But it was two years before we got a divorce. My husband wouldn't give me a divorce until I told him that Ravi and I were going to Mauritius for a holiday, and Prem suddenly decided the time had come to do it. I was still so naive that, when my husband told me not to worry, he would find a lawyer and sort it all out, I just let him go ahead. He told me that when I was asked anything in court, just to agree. He would see that everything was okay, and it would all go much more quickly. So I even stupidly agreed to saying that I would give him custody of the children. He said it was just a formality as he didn't really want them, but eventually what this meant was that he gave me the children but didn't have to pay maintenance for them. Miss Stupid just didn't realise what she was agreeing to!

I still feel angry with him because of the way he acted, as though he was better than and superior to everyone else, and how he manipulated me.

But Ravi offered me a new security and was prepared to take care of the kids. Here we were, eventually, with four kids and everything going fine. Ravi is a teacher; he was the only person working and supporting us all. Things are just so different in my second marriage. I was suddenly my own person and could do things that I wanted to. He doesn't dictate to me. I don't have to make

137

tea all the time, every time he feels like it. He makes his own tea and even does some of the cooking; when I don't feel like it, he will cook. He just lets me be me, without any fuss. Also, the new relationship is so much more stimulating. Even though my first husband was so intelligent, it didn't benefit me. With Ravi there are so many things that we do together and enjoy. My horizons have been broadened so much with things like travelling together. We have been to Mauritius, Israel, Turkey, the Greek Islands, as well as travelled a lot in South Africa. We entertain a lot, talk about art and all sorts of things. Ravi taught me to play scrabble, which I had never played in my life. I started with three-letter words and now I can beat him, although he has a store of words which is quite marvellous. I never feel small or belittled when I ask him something I don't know.

 138

So life has become a learning and growing process. When the kids were more or less grown up, I decided I wanted to train to do something. I saw a correspondence course advertised to train as a teacher and thought, 'That's what I want to do; why don't I go for it?' Which I did. It has proved to be wonderful in my life. I really enjoy teaching; it has given me a sense of independence and let me meet lots of nice new people.

Later, when we had problems, we were able to talk about them and sort things out. So, I feel that we have dealt with the major hurdles in life and that we are going to grow old together, enjoying everything we have, like the children and the grandchildren.

In fact, Ravi and I have known each other most of our lives. He was a cousin who came to the house occasionally when I was a kid, but I didn't take much notice of him. I remember him when he was a student in Durban and I used to go with my mother to his art exhibitions. I was only a teenager and enjoyed them, but I didn't know that even then he fancied me. So, in a sense there has always been something there, but it hadn't come together until we were thrown into each other's company.

All that traditional Hindu ritual is not what makes a marriage work. When I got married to Ravi, I wanted it all to be as simple as possible and

I refused to wear the *thali* marriage string around my neck. I don't wear a ring or a red dot on my forehead either. That doesn't make you married or keep you together; it's something much deeper than that, some deep kind of understanding and caring.

My visits to an ashram

Ujala Satgoor

Ujala Satgoor was born in 1961 in Pietermaritzburg. She is the only daughter of Vidya Satgoor, who is included in this collection. Ujala attended the Raisethorpe High School and then went to the University of Durban Westville where she majored in Hindi and Sanskrit, thereafter completing her Sanskrit Honours degree. In 1990 she qualified as a librarian at the Library School at the University of Cape Town. At present she is based in Pretoria at the Library and Information Association of South Africa (LIASA), managing the South African Leadership Library Project which is aimed at developing leadership skills among managers of library and information services, so transforming librarians from managers to leaders. Spiritually she has embraced the teachings of Sri Sri Ravi Shankar and the Art of Living Foundation.

In 1985 while I was still at the University of Durban Westville, I became involved in the activities of the World Conference on Religion and Peace (WCRP). It is an international inter-faith organisation with its headquarters in Geneva, which encourages people from different religions to come together to examine the universality of religion and human rights. I was invited to become involved in the movement as a representative of the Hindu faith. During that time in South African history, the movement was very interested in the link between religion and political and human rights. It engaged people in dialogue in an attempt to help them understand traditional and cultural values and to identify the common values of all religions, such as love, forgiveness, justice, peace, freedom.

As a representative of the WCRP and as a Hindu woman, I attended the Malibongwe Women's Conference in Holland in 1990. It was sponsored by the Dutch Anti-apartheid Movement, and was designed to bring together exiled women from the then banned ANC to meet with South African women from all aspects of civil society. As women of faith, we were encouraged to look critically at faith, tradition and human rights, which cannot be separated. For me this was very exciting as it was an opportunity to be part of a bigger process than I had ever been involved in before, while meeting such a wide cross-section of women was inspiring. This proved to be a turning point in my life where I embarked on my own spiritual journey and a quest for deeper integration between my beliefs and practices. I also began to look closely at the link between the oppression of women and religion and tradition. This led to my participation in a documentary entitled 'The Other Voices', which addressed the issue of women, religion and violence.

 142

I consider myself very fortunate to have been raised in the Arya Samaj reformed Hindu tradition. From childhood I was imbued with a strong sense of community and social responsibility. I have a keen awareness of my Indian heritage, which gives me a strong sense of identity and confidence, something that has been very important to me. My cultural and language studies at university as well as the mentoring that I received from community elders and visiting scholars from India have strengthened this knowledge. I have always been highly aware of the balance between my Indian heritage and my South African identity. I am very comfortable with the fact that I am South African. I recognise that India is the land of my heritage and have visited the country several times with my parents and friends. But I am always happy to come home to South Africa.

In the early 1990s I was part of a team that was actively involved in setting up the National Hindu Youth Federation, which aimed to assist Hindu youth to rise above language and caste barriers and to look critically at gender, political, economic and development issues. The non-involvement of Hindu organisations in debates around these issues was of concern since it seemed as if Hindu structures would be excluded from being a part of the dynamic changes that were emerging and beginning to take place in our country. We believed it was important for the community to play an active part in the transformation process.

When I became a part of the team which set up the cultural centre and library at the Consulate General of India, Durban, in 1995, this experience further exposed me to the different attitudes towards women, both here in South Africa and in India. It affirmed for me that South African Indian women are much more vocal and critical, and that we challenge tradition far more than our counterparts in India. Women here are much more assertive and feel they have a definite role in social development. We are faced with clearly defined and urgent challenges, and I believe the legacy of legislated segregation has made us value democracy and human rights very highly.

Spiritual journeys are usually precipitated by personal upheavals. Mine was prompted by a marriage and divorce that forced me to question traditional and customary roles and stereotypes within Hinduism. I also began to question the attitudes within organised Hinduism towards women and the double standards that prevailed, even in the supposed reformed tradition such as Arya Samaj. Things like saying to women, 'We want you to be involved on an equal footing,' but leaving women out when decisions are taken. Are women allowed to rise to the highest level? The traditional attitude that religion and politics do not mix is contrary to the values of justice and humanity. The fact that women should not become involved in politics, or should engage within an organisation only at a certain level, contradicts the fact that it is mainly women who are the custodians

143

of tradition and religious practices. As a woman, you may become a successful professional but remain a religious minor!

I cannot accept this narrow mindset and, being imbued with my own sense of identity and worth and an awareness of what I can contribute, I moved away from mainstream Hindu tradition. For me religion means humanity, that there is a purpose for being on this earth. By recognising this, we are able to make a positive difference. It's far more than repeating phrases and doctrine and performing rituals – one must live it. We are here to serve humanity!

I was drawn to the teachings of Sri Sri Ravi Shankar, who established the Art of Living Foundation in 1982, which calls itself an 'education and humanitarian foundation'. It is committed to developing full human potential and fostering human values, and so looks very much at the concept of self-awareness, service to community and humanity, and encourages intense meditative practices. It aims at a balanced lifestyle, leading to a greater balance and harmony of body and mind. It is not about opting out and living the life of an ascetic, but rather being out there in the community and making a concerted difference. It is important to show and lead by example.

 144

The headquarters and ashram of the Art of Living Foundation are situated about 21 km outside the great thriving business centre of Bangalore in Karnataka State, south India. My journey towards becoming an Art of Living teacher included intensive training programmes in South Africa, followed by retreats in India during 1998 and 1999. Subsequently I have run several courses here in South Africa. It is important to embrace the teachings within all aspects of one's life. Professionally, it has enabled me to be focused and disciplined; personally, it has enabled me to resolve issues and move on with my life.

I visited the ashram for the first time in December 1998 when I was invited to participate in the teacher training programme, an intense 15-day programme. I had flown from South Africa to Mumbai with my friend and soul sister Anithra Jadoo, and then we caught the train to Bangalore, a 24-hour journey. My first impression when I arrived at the ashram after the exhausting long journey was a sense of belonging and 'coming home'. I immediately felt very welcome and at peace, with a sense of great nurturing. The pressures of travel, personal issues and spiritual uncertainties seemed to evaporate. The concern for one's well-being and comfort by the ashramites was most warming.

The grounds of the ashram are particularly beautiful. They spread over 24 acres, which incorporate several hills and a lake and are planted with many types of trees. A previously barren piece of land has been transformed into a haven of greenery, and is regarded as an example of how we can bring about transformation through our efforts. A series of pathways leads one through the grounds to the hills and the lake. Even though the national highway is not far away, one feels far from the hustle and noise of city life, and surrounded by a deep feeling of peace and serenity which contributes to the aim of relieving tension and stress. In keeping with the Foundation's commitment to re-establishing balance and living in accordance with the rhythms of nature, the campus has been designed to be in harmony with the natural environment. Organic farming is practised, growing fruits such as bananas and papayas, as well as tomatoes, potatoes, okra, rice and *raagi*. There is also an extensive herb garden. No artificial fertilizers or pesticides are used, and all the wonderful vegetarian food cooked in the ashram comes from the farm. Solar panels are used to generate power for water pumps, heating and lighting, and bio-gas is generated from organic waste and used for cooking.

The numerous buildings such as the meditation halls, residences known as *kutirs* (Sanskrit for 'house' or 'residence'), and amphitheatres, have all been built according to traditional Indian architecture to maintain the natural harmony of the environment. The meditation hall, of course, is very important as all the meditation courses are conducted here. Just recently, because of the increasing number of people coming to the ashram, a new and much larger meditation hall is being constructed with five storeys, which can accommodate two thousand people in the two lower levels. Men and women participate together in all the activities of the ashram.

The Sumeru Mantap, the marriage canopy, is a circular building at the highest point of the ashram grounds with a wonderful view over the garden and the surrounding countryside. It is an unusual-looking but attractive structure in

145

the shape of a lotus with twelve pillars to represent the sun signs. It provides a marvellous setting for those who choose to hold their wedding celebrations here.

There is also an amphitheatre which is used for outdoor gatherings, often at night. When sitting on the grass, one is able to appreciate the starry sky above.

The ashram has two shops, one selling books and audio and video cassettes on a variety of themes of interest to ashramites, while the other provides practical items such as soap and toothbrushes, as well as things like saris, *dhotis* and incense.

The Ayurveda Clinic provides wonderful treatments and therapies according to the principles of this ancient indigenous Indian medical system. Here various herbal preparations are made such as body wash, shampoo, healing creams and herbal teas, which are for sale. You can have a most relaxing massage in these peaceful surroundings with pastes made from spices such as turmeric and sandalwood to cleanse and nurture your skin, causing the stresses and strains to melt away. A special regime of treatments will be designed specially for you to bring a harmony of mind, spirit and body, accompanied by wholesome and delicious vegetarian food. One is given advice on how to modify one's diet to achieve a more balanced life.

 146

The ashram also has a publications division which produces books and newsletters on the beliefs and work of the Foundation, a well-stocked library, and a computer centre that deals with the enormous volume of mail from people all round the world.

My first room, circular in shape, consisted of six beds and an attached bathroom. Once we started the training programme, we were moved to a dormitory – an instant lesson in the dropping of barriers and personal comfort zones.

There is a daily regime of activities based on the principles of *seva* (service), *sadhana* (spiritual practices) and *satsangh* (communal worship). It begins at 6 a.m. with everyone gathering in the meditation hall for *asanas* (yogic postures) and *sadhana*, spiritual practices such as breathing and chanting, designed to awaken awareness of our connections with the rhythms of nature and to effect a profound inner transformation. This is followed by a simple breakfast of fruit and milk. All in residence are expected to do some form of *seva*, for example kitchen duties such as chopping vegetables, rolling out *chappatis*, or working in the garden. *Satsangh* is held daily after dinner. This is the communal worship and coming together of believers, which is the highlight of the day and a very joyous time with the singing of *bhajans* and listening to a talk or sermon, the sharing of knowledge by *Guruji* or other spiritual teachers. It is also a time for dialogue where one can ask questions and initiate discussion. *Guruji* is noted for imparting profound knowledge simply, and with a sense of humour.

When *Guruji* is in residence, he holds a daily *darshan* at 4.30 p.m., which is an opportunity to enjoy his powerful presence. Many people, even from outside the ashram, come for this special occasion. Crowds of devotees throng to offer him flower petals and to receive his blessing as he walks among the people and listens to their problems and requests. He ensures that he meets all who attend residential programmes at the ashram. I found it wonderful, and at times extremely amusing, to observe how people become childlike in his presence.

One of the most amazing observations for me was the stillness I experienced in that environment and in the presence of *Guruji* – the chattering of the mind actually stopped. It's certainly not a feeling of loss of control, but rather a deep feeling of quietude and stillness. He is so charismatic and does not use rhetoric. He is a man of few words who is highly committed to social upliftment and believes that living one's faith is all important. The concept of *seva* is central to this: social service and support for the needy with both material and spiritual comfort. Service to humanity brings spiritual growth.

My time at the ashram also helped me to experience the 'colour' of Hinduism in a way I had never been aware of before. I came to appreciate just how multifarious Hinduism is, how full of emotion and devotion it is, not just the intellectual aspects I had been trained in. I needed to experience faith and devotion at a very personal level, in the heart, rather than always seeking a rational explanation in the head. Sometimes you merely have to feel and experience. For me it's about the balance between doing the rituals and the concentration on the inner, meditative aspects.

The Foundation makes a point of treating women and men equally. We women are treated as individuals in our own right; our spiritual growth is dictated by our

147

own choices, and we have the right to access any information and knowledge. Knowledge is not exclusive to males and all go through the same training programmes. This is one of the important aspects that attracted me to this way of life. Progress is self-paced so you move at your own speed, when you are ready.

Sri Sri Ravi Shankar does a lot of international travelling to promote his teachings and engage with other international organisations committed to humanitarian values. He has appointed teachers in over 140 countries to work locally. Here in South Africa we have 26 teachers in the ART EXCEL children's programmes, the adult programme Prison Smart for the rehabilitation of prisoners, and the 'Breath, Water, Sound' programme offered in townships to help people de-stress and recognise the negative impact of stress on their lives.

The Foundation places great emphasis on one's purpose in life – each person is here to make a difference to his or her world, contributing and engaging with other people constructively. Recognition of this makes life worthwhile.

 148

Professionally, my spiritual commitment serves as a great foundation for my life. I see my current work as the Project Co-ordinator of the South African Library Leadership Project as a great challenge for the betterment of our country. We participate in a partnership project between the Library and Information Association of South Africa (LIASA) and the Mortenson Center for International Library Programs at the University of Illinois, USA. It aims to develop leadership among senior and middle managers of library services in South Africa. Our focus areas are leadership, change management and organisational structures, advocacy and communication, and current best practices in library management. This training is conducted at the University of Illinois over a period of six weeks. So far, during 2002 and 2003, we have taken 16 South Africans there to benefit from this programme, where they have been exposed to various innovative ideas and projects that are all committed to social upliftment and integration.

When I was in New York in 2002, we visited the Queensborough Public Library, one of the largest public library systems in the United States and renowned for its services to immigrants. It has over 65 active language collections comprising books, newspapers, magazines and journals, as well as audio-visual material in a particular language. The staff who run these centres have had considerable professional training. These libraries have become community centres, the first stop for new immigrants who need to learn how to access the local government system and benefits available to them in their new country, such as social security, hospital services, social welfare and educational facilities. Job or career centres and English literacy classes with qualified personnel are available. Computer centres, childcare and school homework facilities and supervision are included in the services provided. Libraries are beginning to recognise their role in social responsibility, rather than merely performing their former recreational role. I find it exciting that a librarian's job no longer consists of maintaining rows of neat shelves and stamping and issuing books.

Working within the information and library services, one is responsible for the development of people's minds. We need to contribute to an informed and socially responsible society. This means working towards the combating of illiteracy, empowering people to read and make decisions for themselves, to create a sense of worth in all people so they are able to say, 'It is my right to read', 'I can be informed', 'It is my right to know'. Libraries need to be redefined to become the hub of a community, people's first stop on the road to integration into society. This is redefining the question of what it means to be informed and how to use this information.

I feel very enthused and proud to be a part of this transformation process. It is extremely challenging but fulfilling, and I am constantly aware of the depth of my spiritual foundation. This allows me to function effectively and to the best of my capabilities. The power of the spiritual practices of my faith permits me to recharge my batteries regularly. However, the thought of returning to the ashram or participating in a retreat is always a priority for me, and I hope to do so soon.

At this stage in my life, I am very comfortable with the choices I have made and the person that I am. I celebrate that I have been given the gift of this opportunity to redefine my life.

149

Identity crisis

Nivashni Nair

Nivashni Nair was born in Pietermaritzburg in 1980. She completed matric at the Dunveria Secondary School and went on to study journalism at the M L Sultan Technikon in Durban. She started her journalism career at the South African Press Association (SAPA) in Durban before being transferred to its Johannesburg office. Nivashni then worked at the Mid South Coast Mail before joining The Witness *office in Durban as a senior journalist. Her interests include writing short stories for children, poetry, spending time with her family, and investigating hard news items. She is currently one of only a thousand journalists in the world to hold the prestigious Development Journalism Diploma, and is the latest recipient of the Rajasthan Pratika Award. A shorter version of this story appeared in* The Weekend Witness *on 27 January 2007.*

At first the stares did not bother me. I attributed them to my 'tourist' look. Of course, anyone with a video camera round her neck, a small 35 mm camera in one hand and a big map of India in the other, and dressed like she came straight out of a travel clothing advertisement, would be stared at.

And then the day that changed my life forever arrived. I didn't understand it. I was dressed in traditional Indian wear, performing the Hindu rituals at a temple on the holy day that Lord Krishna was born, yet people were still staring at me. I asked my Indian friend what was the curiosity surrounding me – after all, there was nothing different about me. I looked Indian. I am a Hindu. I follow many of the traditions.

His reply was that I was not Indian. He said people stared at me because, although I did not realise it, I did look different. He said besides my accent being different, my mannerisms were notably different from people living in India.

 152

It was then that it dawned on me that I was not Indian. Now, two months after returning from my four-month stay in India, I have finally accepted my true identity.

In all honesty, I never really had the desire to visit India although it was where my great-grandparents came from. I always considered myself a South African, while embracing Indian culture and traditions. So when the Indian government nominated me to represent South Africa at the prestigious Development Journalism Fellowship in India, I was excited at the thought of meeting other Indians. But I was nervous about retracing my great-grandparents' lives.

My first interaction with Indians was strange. In fact, it brought many smiles to people back home in South Africa. I walked into a classroom of first-year journalism students at the Indian Institute of Mass Communication in New Delhi and was asked by a curious student which country I was from. Startled that he did not assume I too was Indian, I quickly replied 'South Africa'. The entire group of students looked at me wide-eyed. I felt like I was on display at a museum and, to avoid the silent tension, I looked away. Finally one student plucked up the courage to ask me if I was Black or White. This time my jaw dropped to the ground. In my entire existence I was never asked such a question. Clearly one could see I was

Indian. I responded that I was neither, and that my great-grandparents were from Kerala, the southern tip of India.

'Oh, so you are a person of Indian origin. When I first saw you I thought you were a NRI (non-resident Indian),' someone said. I asked about the difference and was told that I had no claim to India and it was even surprising that I regarded myself as an Indian. I was also told that a NRI was someone who was born in India but had emigrated.

In a confused state I went through the first month in India wondering where I fitted in. All my life I had prided myself on being a South African Indian with links to India. However, the general response to me in India was that I did not have any links to the people in India. I would often get asked about my family history, but it was not as often as when people would sneer at me.

I clearly remember the day when a group of men stared at me in the foyer of the hostel where I was staying. I then asked my Indian friend what they were saying about me in Hindi. 'They are disgusted. They are saying that you are Indian but you want to be European and that you talk like Europeans,' he replied.

That was a turning point. I decided to embrace my culture, only it was not an Indian culture. It was a South African culture. I introduced my foreign friends to the delights of my country and became so obsessed with being a good ambassador that I once even shocked myself when I boasted about our tax system, which funds 'our ever developing infrastructure'.

Despite fully embracing my status as a South African, I still felt that something was missing. I then decided to take a historical journey to Kerala to discover my roots. Upon arriving on the southernmost tip of India, known worldwide as 'God's own country', I felt anxious. There was so much I wanted to know about, yet I did not know where to begin. I met a friend whom I had known for years and I was quickly informed of my status as a 'Nair'. I grinned as I was told about my privileges as a Nair. Now when I think about his words, I still find myself in disbelief. 'As a Nair you are of a noble family and caste. You are different from others and you will be given so many opportunities, but you must always fight to keep our name alive. It's almost like royalty,' he said.

The shock of such a statement was not as severe as the next shock I received. I was surprised when my friend called to ask me if his relative, a journalist, could interview me for the local newspaper. I was honoured as I assumed that perhaps people were intrigued and wanted to discover how people of Indian origin live in South Africa. I was wrong. The newspaper wanted to run an article on me because I was a Tamil-speaking Nair.

I was surprised. Actually, I was shocked. I didn't think it was newsworthy that a Nair was Tamil-speaking as I did not think of it as being unusual. However, I was told differently. 'You should change. Your language is supposed to be Malayalam. Tamils and Malayalams don't get on. They even had a physical war. Being a Tamil is wrong for a Nair,' the journalist said.

After the most confusing meeting of my life, I went to my hotel room and phoned my father back home in South Africa. He too was surprised, and reassured me that being Tamil-speaking was not a sin. He explained that when my great-grandparents came to South Africa, they were a minority in the Indian community. 'So, in order to fit into a community, they became Tamil-speaking, but they never forgot that they came from Kerala and they tried their best to remind us of their roots,' he said.

In the last month of my journey, I finally accepted all that I had learnt about being an Indian, or a person of Indian origin. I accepted it, but decided that I – alone – needed to make a decision on who I am. A day before I left, I was presented with the Rajasthan Pratika Award for second position out of thirteen countries and was asked to say a few words. I thought about it and then found the words.

'I came to India to follow in my great-grandfather's footsteps but instead I forged my own path. It was a path that I took as a South African. I accept who I am, and will always be grateful for a fascinating link to Indian culture, but while I look like an Indian, my heart will always be South African.'

Breaking the silence

Padmani Naidoo

Padmani (Pat) Naidoo has been participating in the local Tamil fire-walking ceremony for the goddess Draupadi for many years. As a devotee of the goddess Kali, she has also been involved in numerous other festivals and religious activities. The story of her religious commitment is told further on in this anthology. However, unbeknown to most people, she was involved in a most painful, parallel experience at the same time, which is recorded here. Since her divorce she has chosen to revert to her family name of Naidoo.

I lived in Mount Edgecombe until, when I was fifteen, I met Reuben Pillay who was seventeen. Soon after that, in 1973, we got married according to Hindu rites and came to Maritzburg to live in Northdale. For two years we were very happy, really very excited about being married, and Reuben got a job at Northdale hospital as a porter.

At that time I had very long hair that was down to below my knees, which I had grown for Mother Kali as I was devoted to her. I was very involved at the temple in Longmarket Street and took part in a lot of festivals. It was all highly rewarding, and I felt accepted there and met many good people. There was much friendliness and support from other devotees.

Then, after about two years, Reuben started getting jealous because I was so often involved with things at the temple. He was worried by my long hair as he thought that other men would come running to me, and take me away from him. He felt threatened by my hair and kept saying he didn't like it. So one morning I was in the kitchen cooking because his family were coming for a meal, and we were expecting 13 people for lunch. I had washed my hair and, while it was drying, I put it up in a loose bun instead of plaiting it as I usually did. While I was stirring the food in a big pot, bending over the wood stove, he suddenly grabbed me, loosened my hair, and pushed my head down to the flame so my hair caught fire. It all burnt before I could put it out, and my neck was badly burnt – I still have the scar, here on the side of my neck and chest. The top of my legs were also burnt because my hair was so long, and my clothes were burnt as well, but luckily not my face as I had tried to hide it from the flames. As soon as I could, I ran to the shower to put out the fire.

I was terribly shocked and in great pain, but finally when his mom and family came and asked what had happened to my hair, I had to lie to them. I told them it just fell into the coals while I was cooking. I didn't know what to do. All I could think was that I wanted to go home to my mother, but I knew I couldn't because she would feel I was disgracing her name.

I thought of Mother Drobadi [Draupadi] who had been through so much pain when her enemies dragged her by her long hair. She had suffered so much, and I

158

was now suffering – not as much as her, but in the same sort of way. In a way this was comforting to feel I was suffering some of the same pain.

Then in 1977 I lost my mom. She never found out what was happening with Reuben, and after her death I had to look after five of my sisters from then on.

Some time later, in 1978, when my first child Sharon was a year old, Reuben came home very drunk. He sat down and lit a cigarette. Suddenly he just attacked me and started burning me with the cigarette, on my face and my neck. It was terrible, but I went on living with him because of the child.

Sometimes Reuben would lie on the bed with me and start to be loving, and then he would suddenly abuse me. It was dreadful because I knew it was not the way a husband and wife should be. But then I began to get angry.

While I was pregnant with my second child, I was puzzled because one of my sisters developed a large stomach. When I asked her about it, she said she had a growth but I noticed that she was not getting her periods. I had my second child Mergan in June, and in July my sister had a daughter. When I asked her who the father was, she wouldn't tell me, but a bit later she told my brother that it was Reuben's child. When I asked Reuben about this, he hit me so hard that he cracked one of my ribs so I had to go to the hospital. But our relationship carried on. I didn't know Maritzburg well and I didn't know where to go for assistance, so I just put up with it. I had to live with it as I didn't know what to do.

159

Then my youngest sister, my baby sister, got pregnant. She had two children with Reuben. When I said to him, 'Why are you doing this; you mustn't do it!' he hit me. One day he put me in the car, the old Peugeot 404 we had then, and drove up the road to my sister's because he said he wanted me to know that he was having an affair with her; she could acknowledge it and tell me it was true. I started arguing with him and he threw me out of the moving car. I fell on the pavement and cracked my head and hurt my hand. Just then a police van drew up and picked me up and asked me what had happened. They charged Reuben then but, because I didn't go to make a statement, the charge was dropped.

Luckily most of the time he was out with one of his mistresses, and I and the children were alone. I went on attending festivals at the temple, doing all the usual things and putting on a happy face with friends and relatives, trying to make out that all was okay and that my marriage was fine.

Suddenly, one day I got sick with an awful pain in my stomach and I lay on the bed. My little sister came to visit me and gave me some milk to drink. I became very muddled and collapsed. I thought she had put some dope in it. My brother-in-law (Reuben's brother), who was kind to me, came to the house and helped me to bath and took me to Northdale Hospital. The doctor asked why I had taken an overdose and called a social worker. I told her what was happening, the first person I had ever told. We then found that my son's epileptic tablets were missing. My sister and Reuben had been giving these to me. The doctor was kind and helped me. He said I should charge Reuben, but I didn't want to cause any more hurt. When I went home to my brother-in-law, I was very weak and had some fits because of those tablets. He looked after me and took me for some walks to try to get me strong again.

 160

Again I went back home and, on a Friday evening, Reuben arrived when he had just been paid. He was working at Eddels now, but he wouldn't give me any money for food or for the rent. The children went to school without lunch and I couldn't pay the school fees. The children's teacher and the principal were kind and helped them by bringing them lunch and sending food home for us. They told me not to worry about the school fees. I had to sell some of the furniture to get money for food, and when they turned off the electricity I had to cook on a fire outside in the yard.

Reuben, who hadn't been around for a while, then decided to come back and live at home again. One evening he just suddenly got angry and poked me, stabbing me with a three-star Okapi three times in the back. My son ran out and called the neighbours, who rang for the police. They came and called an ambulance. I was taken to Grey's Hospital where they kept me for a while. Reuben had run away because he knew the police were looking for him, but after three days he came back with his niece, who took his side. I called the police again but, before they got there, he ran again. The police called the Child Abuse Unit as they knew he was also hitting and swearing at the children because they had helped me when he attacked me.

A White social worker came and I told her about the stabbing. I also told her that he was raping me, which I had never told anyone before. I couldn't tell the children because I was ashamed, but they overheard what I said and asked if it was true, and I had to say yes. That day the police found Reuben and charged him, and he was told not to come near me. But they never came back, so nothing happened. I don't think they were interested. I never saw that social worker again, and I wonder what happened because nothing really changed.

Often I would be ready to go out to a festival or to do prayers at someone's house and, when the people arrived in their car to fetch me, Reuben wouldn't let me go. If I insisted and went, there would be a problem when I came home. At the end of 1984, he decided he was a Christian and not a Hindu any more. He said the Mother was a devil, which hurt me a lot. When we were fasting and not eating any meat, say for the fire-walking, he would bring meat, especially beef and pork, into the house and cook it.

161

The years passed and the children grew up. When I had been married for 28 years I said, 'I can't cope; I can't take it any more.' I was having bad nerves and I said to the children, 'I'm going to leave because you are all now big.'

So, in April 2001 I packed two bags and went to my sister in Copesville and explained what I was doing. She knew about Reuben and said I could live there, which was a great relief. But after three days Reuben arrived with his Okapi and threatened me again, so I quickly ran out. Reuben said I'd get nothing from the house; he would sell it all. I just said, 'Okay, I came with nothing and I will leave with nothing.'

When I left, the children had stayed in our house with Reuben and I heard that he was always drunk and abusive to them, shouting and swearing at them, saying awful things. So I decided to go back to talk to him. I sat with him on the bed to discuss things with him, and explained that we should try to reconcile and live together. He said okay, he'll try.

I got a job in a clothes shop in Manchester Road because we needed money badly. When I got home from work on the Sunday at 3 p.m., I said I needed a car to fetch the rest of my stuff from Copesville. My son borrowed a car and we went and collected my clothes. When we got home, I saw that Reuben was smoking mandrax. I didn't say anything, but put my things in the bedroom and went to join the children who were playing cards. At 10 p.m. I said I was tired and wanted to go to bed. So I went into the room quietly and undressed, put on my nightie and got into bed, on my side of the bed. Reuben was lying there on his side of the bed and I thought he was asleep. I was very tired, so I dozed off. Suddenly I felt a great jump and Reuben leapt up on the bed and held me down with his knees. I begged him not to hurt me, and said, 'What do you want?' But he just put the radio on very loud so the children couldn't hear and he raped me. It was very painful. Then he slapped me hard, turned me over and stabbed me again with the 'three star'. At first I just felt something piercing me and didn't know what was happening, but then I felt blood and I screamed.

 162

He ran out of the room and the children came out, and he yelled, 'Let the bitch die!' It was about 11.30 p.m. and the children ran out of the house into the street, screaming for help. The neighbours came and some women held me up to try to stop the blood, which was coming out of my mouth. The ambulance and the police arrived and asked what had happened. I just said, 'He poked me with the knife', but I was too embarrassed to say that he had also raped me.

Again they took me to Grey's and my eldest daughter came with me. The police asked the doctor how serious it was, and he said I needed stitches but it wasn't too serious. They sent me home at about 2 a.m., after 22 stitches and an injection for pain. And I slept because I was so exhausted.

The next morning the two older children went to work, my youngest – Rogani – to school, and I was left in the house with my grandchild, my oldest daughter's child, who was four years old. It was so terrible, as I was supposed to be looking after him but he did his best to look after me, so carefully.

Obviously the reconciliation didn't work. Reuben came home later and told me he had been to the police station and made a statement, so I didn't need to see them again. I was so stupid and shocked that I believed him.

A male friend of mine, a teacher, then contacted me to ask if I would come to his house to pray and help to get rid of some evil spirit that was causing a problem there. I said I would help, but I needed money badly. He asked how much, and I said I needed at least R1500 to find somewhere to live, a room somewhere. He gave me R3000 so I could pay for a room with a kitchen and bathroom and have some over for food.

I went home to fetch some of my stuff. Reuben was there and he demanded that I give him some money. I lied and said I had no money. I told him that I was going to see a lawyer, but instead I went to organise for the room. Then I went back to the house and said I needed to take a bed, and he agreed as he was afraid of the police then. So I got the bed there, and I just lay on it and stayed in the room for a long time.

The next morning I borrowed a wheelbarrow and went to my temple at home to fetch my deities, my *murtis* and pictures, to clear out the temple. I put everything in the barrow and had to make three trips to get it all away. I set up my shrine in my room, with my things around me. This made me feel very relieved and strong again.

I stayed there for about a year and the children didn't come to see me in all that time, which made me feel very sad and lonely. Then I heard Reuben was giving them terrible trouble again. My son came to see me, very drunk, and said he had been fighting with his father. He said Daddy slapped Sharon and shouted at Rogani. Mergan blamed me for all that was happening. I went to see Sharon at work and she agreed to come and see me on Sunday for lunch. She spent three hours with me, which was really nice, but we were both afraid Reuben would come and make a whole lot of problems for us. He was drunk when she got home, and he shouted and swore and told them not to see me again.

On Mothers' Day 2005 all the children came to visit me with gifts. This made me so happy and I felt loved again. They told me, 'Mom, do you know you sold the house?' and I said, 'What are you talking about?' They said Daddy had told them and he was selling the house. It turns out he had gone to court and said I was abusive to the children because I was drinking and smoking. He got an interdict that I was not to come to see the children anymore.

So I arranged that we both go to see a magistrate for me to explain my side of the story. I told the magistrate, 'I would never abuse my babies, my precious

163

children. I am a very disciplined person.' And I told him what had happened with Reuben. The magistrate listened and said, 'What would you like to do about the problem?' and I said, 'Shoot him dead!' The magistrate granted me a warrant of arrest that if Reuben came again to worry us, I should call the police and they would lock him up.

I moved to my friends in Jaipur Road because I couldn't pay the rent where I was. At last, in 2002, Reuben applied for a divorce and the sheriff came looking for me to serve the divorce papers. We sat down and I saw how many papers there were, and I was suspicious. So I asked him to read them to me and he said, 'Here, can you read?' And I said, 'No, I can't.' So he read them to me and again Reuben was accusing me of all the trouble and all the bad things, which I told the sheriff wasn't true. He said to me, 'Help yourself. Go and see an attorney.'

So I spoke to a friend, my daughter's ex-husband Richard. He said, 'I can't believe what this is saying. This is not you he is talking about. You couldn't be like this.' He gave me R5 for a taxi to get to town and I went to see a lawyer who I know. I told him the story about the divorce papers and he said, 'I'll handle this. You go home and eat and rest, I'll sort it out.'

I decided to go to my friend Joey's – to his mother's house. I had known them for fifteen years from the temple, especially Joey from the fire-walking in which we both took part. I explained what was happening, that the lawyer was going to help me, and they let me stay there. His mother was wonderful to me.

Finally, in 2003, I got the divorce and it was over. But Reuben is still around and the children see him quite often. He hasn't changed and fights with Sharon, often trying to get money from her.

Joey had been married and had two children, but he was divorced and living with his mother. We were both on our own and in the same position, so one day Joey said, 'Let's live together, get a place together, as we're both alone.' So we asked his mother what she thought, and she said, 'Yes, go ahead, do it.' He went to see his children to tell them. My children were big, but Joey's children were quite small. I was rather worried about them, so I told him to talk to his wife to try to reconcile, but it couldn't be sorted out. His children were happy with him living with me, but my youngest daughter still wanted me to go back to her father.

But Joey and I got a room with family friends in Jaipur Road. We lived there for many months and then got married with Hindu rites. We are now here in this very small place. He is doing work painting houses, and I am still seeing people to help them solve problems with the Mother's blessing. Joey is a wonderful man and does everything he can to make me happy. And his mother is wonderful too, and we see her often. She is a very supportive and loving mother.

My children are all doing well. Sharon has a job, and so does Rogani, who has now left school. Mergan married a Christian woman and they have two little girls, so I have three grandchildren, which is great. They often come to see me here, to spend the day or to sleep over.

I am now experiencing new things, and I'm happy. I didn't really know how to love a person until now, with Joey. He is the best thing that ever happened in my life. We do all our temple work together. Joey is studying with a man near here to be a Brahman priest and is hoping to go to India to continue his training. I would love to go too, but in the meantime Joey is doing lots of the rites, like funerals and the sixteen- and forty-day ceremonies after the funeral, to help in the community.

My hair grew again, but it's never been as long as it was before it was burnt.

165

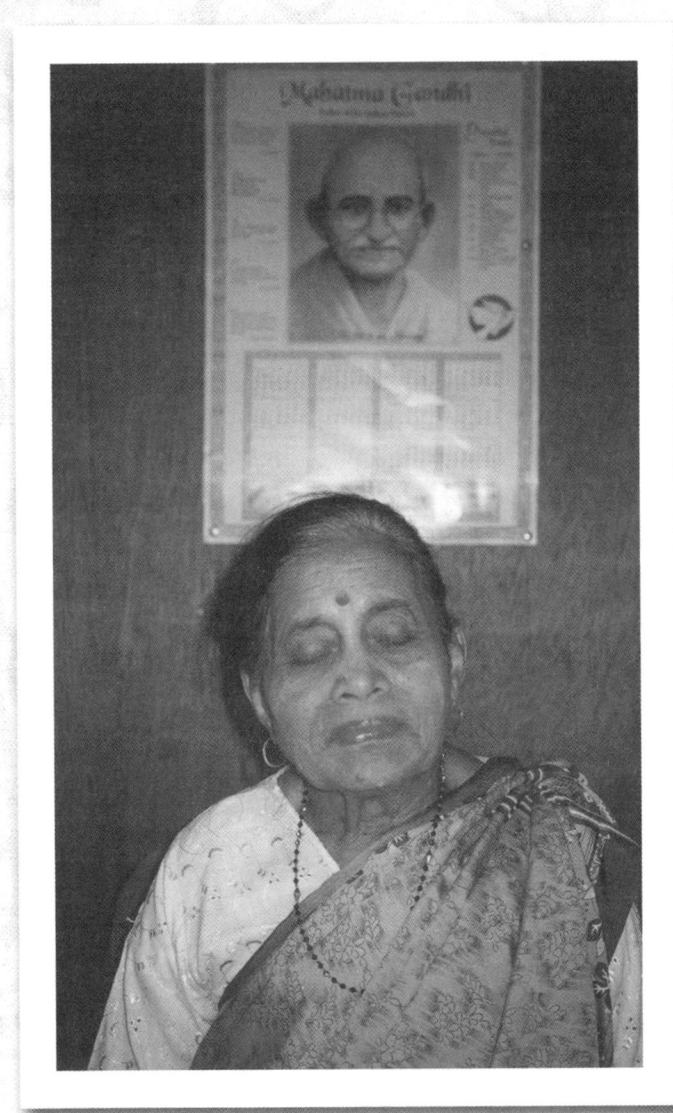

Durga, the invincible warrior for peace

Durga Bundhoo

Durga Bundhoo was born in 1921 in Westville of South African Indian parents, the Satyapauls, who were Hindi-speaking. When she was six months old, her parents moved to Pietermaritzburg where she has lived ever since, becoming involved in a wide variety of service organisations such as the Indian detachment of the Red Cross, the Girl Guides movement, the Pietermaritzburg Child Welfare Society, the Aryan Benevolent Society and, most importantly, the Indian Women's Association. Her commitment to human rights and her sense of civic responsibility have resulted in her quite exceptional contribution to life in the local Indian community, as well as in the wider Pietermaritzburg area. For this reason it is important that her work be recognised and recorded as fully as possible.

Like her namesake, the courageous, beautiful and invincible warrior-goddess Durga, who fought against the demons of chaos and destruction, Durga Bundhoo has spent her life fighting unsparingly against the forces of injustice and prejudice to promote social, political and religious tolerance and liberty. This diminutive, sari-clad figure creates a most powerful impression wherever she goes.

'Life has been so beautiful,' says Durga Bundhoo, on being encouraged to reminisce about her life's experiences.

Some of Durga's earliest memories are of their family home, a cottage in East Street, where she remembers that at one time there were as many as 27 people in the joint family system, but that everyone got along happily with little tension. She describes her mother as 'an illiterate genius', and chiefly remembers her father, who worked as the French polisher at Reid's Cabinet Works in Longmarket Street, as a follower of Mahatma Gandhi and his teachings on peaceful political activism. He was something of a Hindi scholar and wrote a number of plays in the language. They were staunch Arya Samaj supporters, and instilled in Durga very strong values of social service and a dedication to assisting the poor and underprivileged. Durga remembers their home as a meeting place where many political activists gathered, and being visited by several *swamis* from India. In this environment she was frequently exposed to lively and stimulating discussions.

 168

Durga's first school was St Anthony's in Retief Street. From there, in 1935, she went to the newly founded Indian Girls' High School, where she was one of the first scholars. At first the Girls' High School only went to Standard 6, so she had to go on to Woodlands High School where she became the first head girl in her matric year – 1941. She has happy memories of feeling inspired by much of the poetry they studied, and quotes: 'Good people all, of every sort, Give ear unto my song; And if you find it wond'rous short, It cannot hold you long.' And then, together with her husband: 'Lives of great men all remind us, We can make our lives sublime, And, departing, leave behind us, Footprints on the sands of time.'

Durga clearly remembers war breaking out in 1939 while she was in high school. In her matric year, the Committee of the Indian Women's Association approached her to become their treasurer, a great honour, and the beginning of her life-long association with that group. After completing her matric, which was something that few Indian women managed at that time, she went into teaching, strongly encouraged by her parents. She taught at the Methodist government-aided Indian School for five years.

During her time at this school, in 1944, the Red Cross Detachment 83 was formed by the Indian Women's Association in response to fears of the outbreak of an epidemic at the end of the war. This was the first opportunity that Indian girls had to embark on some training as nurses. Durga remembers how, when her sister wanted to become a nurse, she had to go to Middlesex Hospital and then to Guy's Hospital in London to train. So, 36 enthusiastic girls enrolled for the first Red Cross classes. Some of them, including Durga, spent some time helping out in the Indian ward at Grey's Hospital. Many of these young women later went to England to train further and take up nursing as a career. Durga Bundhoo was the commandant of this detachment from 1944 to 1947. One of her most memorable moments during this period was on 18 March 1947, the occasion of the royal visit to Pietermaritzburg. A special event was arranged at the Agricultural Showgrounds in the afternoon to allow the royal party to meet members of the Indian community and to watch a short display by the children. Durga's detachment was asked to do duty. As she stood by the gate to welcome the royal party, the queen (later the Queen Mother) stopped and said to her, 'You must have had a very busy day.' This was certainly true as 14 000 Indians were there to give the king, the queen, and the princesses a most enthusiastic welcome. 'Hah! What a wonderful day that was!' she laughs.

When she married Dasarath Bundhoo in 1947, she left her home in East Street and went to live with his family in Plessislaer. Both Durga and her husband have very happy memories of life in Plessislaer, where a flourishing and vibrant Indian community lived in close and friendly contact with their Black neighbours. If anyone was in trouble, the whole community got together to help. It was 'one big family and no-one could starve there'. Nobody had cars in the early days, so everybody walked wherever they wanted to go. It was so safe that there was no need to lock one's doors. Durga recalls how, whenever Dasarath had to go away, she never felt afraid as she knew the community would look after her. Although many people lived in fairly simple wattle and daub houses, people owned their properties. These were large, with vegetable gardens and cows and chickens, so many families lived mainly off the land. Dasarath's father gave him some land on which, with the help of other members of his family, he was able to build a large brick house with a huge kitchen, a wide passage, and numerous rooms. The Local Health Commission provided light and water.

Because her numerous commitments to various organisations were taking up more and more of her time, Durga decided to give up teaching to devote herself full-time to voluntary work. But there was such a pressing need for teachers that she was persuaded to go back to teach Class 1 at the afternoon session of the Baijoo-Maharaj Platoon School in Raisethorpe. The daily journey from Plessislaer to Raisethorpe involved two buses there and another two home again after work. She spent six years there as principal before she finally gave up teaching to do her social work.

Because she was a teacher at the time, Durga was unable to join the Passive Resistance Campaign organised by the Natal Indian Congress in the 1940s. But she did encourage women from the Indian Women's Association to join and get involved. When a number of people, including some of her relatives, were arrested because of action in Gale Street, Durban, she helped to collect money to support the families. The Bundhoos were always very conscious of being inspired by the life and work of Mahatma Gandhi.

While they were still living in Plessislaer, the Bundhoos were raided by the Security Police who were looking for a typewriter which they believed was the source of a particular political pamphlet. It proved not to be the Bundhoo machine, but Dasarath took the opportunity to engage the policemen in a discussion about the injustice of apartheid. Durga went through to the kitchen to prepare cookies for tea, which they then all shared together. They strongly believed it was their duty to seize every opportunity to bring people of differing political persuasions together.

Tragedy struck the Plessislaer community in 1971 when the Group Areas Act ordered the entire Indian community to move out and resettle in Northdale, on the other side of Maritzburg, without any compensation. The Bundhoos

❀ 170

were part of a group of protesters who attempted to resist the move, demanding an alternative scheme where everyone received some reparation. This finally ensured that each household got some payment, however inadequate, for their property. The Bundhoos refused to leave Plessislaer until they had seen everyone else re-housed. But the heartbreak of leaving well-established homes and smallholdings was exacerbated by the fact that the plots and houses in Northdale were too small to accommodate extended families who had lived together for generations, thus forcing separation and its accompanying suffering on many people, especially the elderly. People were also separated from their places of worship so new temples had to be built.

The only consolation that the Bundhoos have from this awful time in their lives, they say, is the fact that a place of learning, the Indumiso College, was built on the site of their house.

Most of Durga Bundhoo's social work has sprung from her involvement with the Pietermaritzburg Indian Women's Association, which was formed in 1933. The inspiration for this organisation came from Kunwar Rani Maharaj Singh, the wife and secretary of the Indian agent-general in South Africa from 1933 to 1935. She was asked to address a meeting of the Pietermaritzburg Indian Parliamentary Debating Society in the library of the Hindu Young Men's Association (HYMA) one evening in August 1933. On looking round at her audience, Kunwar Rani was dismayed to see only two women. On asking where the women were, she was told that Indian women did not go out in public because they couldn't read or write. When she enquired further whether there was an Indian women's club where she might go to relax from the demands of her work, she was told there was no such thing. So it was that Kunwar Rani encouraged the local Indian women to found an association where they could meet, exchange ideas, achieve literacy in the English language, become involved in welfare work, and generally make progress in, and contribute to, South African society.

After much canvassing, in September of that year a large group of Indian women assembled in the HYMA hall, along with officials from the White National Council of Women who were there in an advisory capacity because

Indian women had gained so little experience of organising and participating in public activities. Mrs Eleanor Russell (who later became the first woman mayor of Pietermaritzburg) was installed as the founding president, with other White women on the committee. The initial aim of the Association was to bring together Hindu, Muslim and Christian Indian women to work for the improvement of their lives through literacy and general education, thus encouraging them to become more active and responsible in their community and the society into which they were born.

At this time there was no opportunity for high school education for Indian girls, which resulted in widespread illiteracy. One of the initial projects of the newly formed Association, therefore, was to persuade the Natal Education Department to build the Indian Girls' High School in Berg Street. This was started in 1935, with the primary section housed in the HYMA hall. The Woodlands High School for boys was also opened to girls.

 172

After five years, when the White committee saw that the Association was firmly launched, they transferred their portfolios to Indian women. The dynamic Mrs Leah Zachariah becoming the first president, a position she held for twenty years.

So pleased was Kunwar Rani with the achievements of the Indian Women's Association that, on addressing their annual general meeting just before she returned to India in 1935, she said: 'All those of you born in South Africa must learn to serve and love the country of your birth. The women of India were given the vote, but it is sad that the Indian men in South Africa are voteless. It is imperative therefore for the Indian women of South Africa to join their menfolk to achieve full citizenship rights. Wake up, and keep waking up!'

In 1935 the Indian Women's Association became affiliated with the National Council of Women of South Africa. They assisted in achieving improvements in the Indian community, such as the removal of the tax on rice and the repeal of the government Act which prohibited the movement of Indians from one province to another. After her initial involvement in the Association in her matric year of 1941, Durga became the representative of the Association on the local National Council executive, a position she held for many years. Later she became the vice-president of the Maritzburg branch of the National Council of Women, the first woman of another race group to hold this position. For six years she held the National Council of Women portfolio of National Advisor for Asian Affairs, which involved monitoring laws passed by the government that affected Indians, particularly women, and advising what further research or action needed to be taken in connection with these laws.

Over the years, the Indian Women's Association became increasingly involved in political matters. These included taking up complaints about the inferior type of housing being built in Northdale, and the need for the establishment of a hospital to serve the area, which eventually resulted in the building of Northdale Hospital.

In order to help foster a stronger sense of their Indian identity in the local community, the Indian Women's Association organised the celebration of India Independence Day in 1947, mourned the assassination of Mahatma Gandhi in 1948, and commemorated the centenary of the arrival of Indian settlers in Natal in 1960.

173

Durga relates how, on 14 January 1947, after a massive cloudburst, the Msinduzi and Dorp Spruits caused devastation by bursting their banks and sweeping through the Indian areas of lower Boom, Greyling, and East Streets, as well as Victoria Road, inundating and destroying many homes. Hundreds of people's homes were completely washed away. The Indian Women's Association co-operated with the Mayor's Relief Fund and stepped in to relieve the situation by providing the destitute victims with groceries, clothing, mattresses and blankets. They also assisted the Camps Drift market gardeners whose crops were flooded by the Msinduzi River every year.

During the treason trials of the early 1980s held in the Umgeni Court in College Road, Durga helped to raise money for, and give comfort to, the families of the detainees. She laughs as she remembers how 'I became a perpetual beggar on the streets of Maritzburg.'

Else Schreiner, with whom Durga worked in the National Council of Women for many years, tells this story, which shows how Durga's outwardly gentle and considerate demeanour hides a tough core. 'Many years ago, in the early 1970s, when Mrs Bundhoo was in the house alone, she answered a knock on her door to find herself confronted by two large members of the much feared Security Branch who told her they had come to search her home. Did she shiver and give in? Oh no, not a bit. She told them that she knew she could not stop them, but she gave them a dire warning. If, she said, they untidied her house, left papers lying around and made a mess, she would immediately phone the press and get them to come and take photographs. Furthermore, she said, the house was to be just as neat and clean as they found it. And, my goodness, she enjoyed watching them! They opened a desk drawer, took the papers out one by one, read them, and put them face down on the desk. Then, when they had finished that drawer, they carefully put everything back and asked her if that was alright. And so it went on for the next and the next and the next bit of their search. Lastly, they went into Mrs Bundhoo's bedroom. One can almost smell their shame as the tiny Mrs Bundhoo drew herself up to her full height and snapped at them: 'Are you not ashamed of yourselves, a big pair of men like you, searching through my drawers, hunting through my clothes and my underclothes? What would your mothers say? Hah! This is disgusting!' Mrs Bundhoo rejoiced inside as those two big men blushed dark red with embarrassment as they apologised to her, but nevertheless said, 'But lady, we have to do it hey.' She stood right next to them. She snorted and told them to tidy up – which they did, probably to their own great surprise. When they had finished that, one of them looked under the bed and saw a small trunk. He hooked his foot through the handle and was about to pull it out when Mrs Bundhoo said, 'Hah! Now you stop. That trunk is full of National Council of Women papers. There is NOTHING in there for you. You leave it alone.' 'But', they said, 'we have to search everything.' 'I'm warning you that if you open that trunk I will call the press, and I will phone the National President of the National Council of Women and tell her what you have done. Hah! Don't you dare open that trunk!' And the men looked at each other and at this furious little woman, and they carefully pushed the trunk back under the bed and went away. This was a triumph of courage and outraged justice over the evil forces.'

As president of the Indian Women's Association, one of Durga's early contributions to reconciliation between racial groups, at the height of the apartheid

174

states of emergency, was to address White Women's Institutes and church groups on subjects such as Hindu religion, Indian cooking, and the wearing of a sari. 'I tried to do whatever it took to spread understanding.'

The chief motivation for all Durga's social concern is her continuing religious commitment to the reformed Hindu group, the Arya Samaj, which she learned from her parents and shares with her husband. For fifty years, since 1948, she has been president of the Plessislaer Arya Stree Samaj women's group, which moved from Plessislaer to Northdale to continue its work in encouraging the education and upliftment of women. In this group, Durga helped to organise literacy and sewing and knitting classes as part of her life-long determination to improve women's quality of life.

In recognition for her contribution to the furtherance of Aryan principles, Durga was invited to represent South Africa at the International Conference of the Arya Samaj in Mauritius in 1973, and then to attend the Arya Samaj Centenary Celebrations in New Delhi in December 1975. A *Natal Witness* article on her return from these centenary celebrations records her experience. Thousands of people from all over the world were there. The theme was 'The Way to World Peace' and the part the Arya Samaj could play in helping to achieve this, something that has always been very close to Durga's heart. She also described how, on the day after the official opening of the conference, 'a procession of some two million marchers was held through the streets of Delhi. The procession, led by *swamis* seated on elephants and others on horseback, is something I shall never forget.' She found the whole experience highly enriching and inspirational. In 1985 she was invited to be the keynote speaker at the Women's Session of the International Conference held in Durban.

An incident which perfectly illustrates Durga Bundhoo's courage and social and political commitment is related to the nationwide student protests and school boycotts of 1982. The security forces reacted harshly. Many students were jailed all over the country, and some were killed. In the Northdale area, over a thousand students at the Woodlands School – who had stood in silent protest – had been attacked by police dogs, and some had been injured and had to be hospitalised.

The next morning news reached the Bundhoos that the pupils at the Esther Payne Smith School in Bombay Road, just down from the Bundhoo's house, had come out in protest and that the Riot Squad had arrived at the school. Durga knew at once that there would be trouble. Her immediate reaction was that she and some other mothers should go down there at once to attempt to defuse the situation. While she hurriedly tied on her sari, she called to her sister-in-law to phone around to tell the other women that she was going to the school. Before leaving the house, Durga went into her bedroom and prayed. The message was passed on very quickly and all the women marched down the road to the school. There were a number of huge police Saracens parked in the road outside the school, and about fifty members of the Riot Squad, armed with guns, had surrounded the school. The teachers stood nearby in silence. Durga led the women into the playground where there was a very tense standoff between a large group of chanting children and the riot police. The teacher at the gate said, 'Do you know what you are doing Mrs Bundhoo?' She answered, 'Leave me alone,' and went to stand next to the headmaster. An inner voice told her, God is on your side. One false move at that stage and the police dogs would have been released. Durga then asked the principal if she could address the children. The principal in turn approached the chief of the riot squad, seated in his vehicle, who spoke to his superior on his radio informing him that this woman wished to address the pupils. It was agreed that she could speak, so the diminutive woman faced the crowd and said, 'Children, will you listen to me?' The tension was broken. The children clapped and clapped, and at this moment she knew she had won their confidence. So she told them they must now disperse and go back to their classrooms one by one, and from there she and the other mothers would take them home. The children obeyed, and the explosive situation was defused. The security forces moved away quietly. Thinking back on this incident, Durga Bundhoo laughingly says, 'I think that was the greatest achievement of my life.'

 176

On another more domestic occasion, Durga once again demonstrated her peace-keeping talent. Two women neighbours erupted into a ferocious quarrel about a chicken that had flown into the wrong yard. One of the women was brandishing a cane knife and screaming, 'I'm going to chop you!' Durga quietly walked over and said, 'Sister, give that to me.' The angry woman was so deflated that she handed it over as the men stood watching, open-mouthed. Then all the involved parties went inside and had a cup of tea.

Durga, together with Dasarath, has been an active member of the Gandhi Memorial Committee in Pietermaritzburg. They played a major role in the erection and unveiling of the Gandhi statue in the Church Street Mall in 1993 on the occasion of the centenary celebrations of Gandhi's eviction from the train on Pietermaritzburg Station.

In 1994 Durga was awarded a citation by the Natal Indian Congress 'to record the outstanding contribution made by Mrs D Bundhoo in the struggle for liberation and human dignity in South Africa through the ranks of the Natal Indian Congress'.

At the Civic Award Ceremony in the Pietermaritzburg City Hall on 17 February 2000, Durga Bundhoo finally received city-wide recognition for her enormous contribution to the life of Pietermaritzburg. A citation was read out which contains an impressive list of her social, educational, political and religious achievements. Her humility is illustrated by her comment in an interview with *The Natal Witness* in which she says that, during the reading of the citation, she thought about how she was receiving this on behalf of 'my mothers and sisters; of all women' (*The Natal Witness*: 29 February 2000).

Durga's life, which spanned most of twentieth century Pietermaritzburg's turbulent history, has been characterised by her quiet determination and courage, and a sense of justice that has been roused unfailingly by all forms of discrimination and deprivation. For over six decades she has been an inspiration and role model to countless women in her home town and much further afield.

177

Hindu women worshipping the goddess in KwaZulu-Natal
Introduction

Hinduism, uniquely among the world religions, preserves the practice of envisioning and venerating divinity in female form. The many Hindu goddesses fall into two categories: consort goddesses who are largely dependent on males for their identity, such as Sarasvati, wife of the male deity Brahma, and Laxshmi, wife of Vishnu. These figures are generally benign, gentle and subservient. Then there are the independent, 'virgin' goddesses, such as Kali, Durga, and the south Indian deities like Mariamman, Draupadi, Angalamman, and Gangaiamman, who are free of male control, characterised by their autonomous strength, and a challenge to patriarchal norms. The term 'virgin' as used to describe these female divinities does not mean sexual inexperience or inactivity. It refers to their undominated and autonomous state, not defined by any sexual relationship with men. It is these independent goddesses who are most popularly worshipped, particularly for their powers of protection and healing.

In KwaZulu-Natal, the worship of the goddess is a popular and high-profile part of Hindu practice. Both women and men are involved in this on an ongoing daily basis, and as participants at various annual festivals. However, women play a particularly prominent role and far outnumber men at some festivals.

Some of the most important and frequent features of these festivals are, first, the taking of vows where devotees vow that if illness or misfortune is overcome, they will participate in a festival or perform some austerity a specified number of times. Severe consequences are believed to follow the breaking of a vow. Second, various austerities are frequently performed to demonstrate devotion to the goddess or some other deity. The most usual of these include fasting, sticking pins and hooks through the body, and walking across fire. Third, there is the trance, where devotees claim to become possessed by a deity, usually one or other of the fierce goddesses such as Kali, the black goddess; Mariamman, goddess of pox diseases; or Draupadi, goddess of fire-walking. Women mostly appear to be possessed by one of the fierce goddesses, and display wild behaviour not normally tolerated in a respectable Hindu woman. It would appear that women experience possession more frequently than men, and that men are more often possessed by one of the male deities, rather than by a goddess.

 180

The triggers for entering a trance state are usually drumming, clapping, chanting, and the smell of burning incense and camphor. People about to become possessed often start trembling, their eyes sometimes roll back, and women with long hair loosen their bun and throw their arms out, while twisting their bodies. Some women shriek loudly as the goddess takes control of them. These women frequently behave in fairly fierce and frightening ways, with large staring eyes, advancing on people, grunting and gesticulating, as they swirl and dance ecstatically. Obviously in some alternate mode of consciousness, they do not seem to feel pain when needles are inserted through their tongues and cheeks, and hooks with garlands attached to them are pinned through the flesh of their chests and backs. Although they lose some sense of awareness, they retain some connection with their surroundings in that they do not walk into objects, are able to recognise people, and are appropriately centred on the main activities of the festival or rituals. This state might be maintained for a few minutes, or for several hours, some people going in and out of the trance state several times during a festival day.

Possessed people are regarded as divine and are much revered, their supernatural powers enabling them to act as oracles, to bless others, and very often to heal. Miracles of healing, and possession itself, are believed to be highly special manifestations of the power of the goddess. A queue of devotees frequently forms in front of a possessed person, waiting to prostrate themselves at her feet and be blessed with a dot of ash placed on their foreheads. Most people do not speak while they are possessed and, of course, a needle through the tongue prevents this. But they communicate with gestures to those who stand before them. Many people who regularly enter into trances at festivals have attained considerable respect and status in the community. Those who 'get trances' claim to experience total amnesia afterwards about the details of the trance state.

It is probably true to say that women in general do not benefit from a higher status in societies where female divinities are revered. But it can be claimed that worship of the goddess can bring some sense of empowerment to individual women devotees.

Here follows accounts of five traditional Hindu women who worship and serve the goddess, whom they normally refer to as 'the Mother', *Sati* (literally meaning 'faithful', a generic name for goddesses) or *Shakti*.

Mrs Singh, the temple auntie

'When I went to Grey's Hospital to have my youngest daughter, I was very sick and I died. I came to a very big river and there was an old lady sitting there. I crossed the river and saw a beautiful, big house with grass all around, and lots of flowers in the garden, and I wanted to stay there for ever. I went inside the house and there were a lot of men, White men and Indian men, sitting in the lounge reading holy books. One of them took a book out and said to me, "See here, in this book; I am not calling you yet. You must go back." I said, "I don't want to go back." But he said, "It is not your time. Who will look after your children?" But I didn't want to go. The next morning I woke up in hospital, and there were doctors all round my bed. The doctor said, "You've been dead all night. We were about to put you in the mortuary cold room." Then the baby was born, but she didn't breathe. So I said, "Dropathi Mater [Mother Draupadi], if she comes alive, she is your child." After one hour she started breathing. I stayed in the hospital a long time and then got better and went home. I already died, so I'm not afraid to die. I can help other people when they are dying by bringing ash from the temple to their beds, and putting it on their heads, their necks, their arms and chests. Then I bless them, which stops their suffering and helps them to die quickly.'

When I interviewed Mrs Singh (as she introduced herself to me), she was about 60 years old and, for some years, had acted as full-time priest/*pujari*, locally known as the 'temple auntie' at one of the oldest of the traditional temples in

Pietermaritzburg. For twenty years before this she used to help out there whenever she was needed. She explained that she had received no formal instruction as a priest and couldn't remember how she learned to do the rituals, but 'God just gave me the power'. Traditional Hinduism does not permit women to become priests, so it is unusual to find a woman in this position. The only reason why Mrs Singh was allowed to perform these priestly duties is that she was post-menopausal and so no longer suffered from the ritual pollution associated with menstruation.

Mrs Singh is from a Hindi background and speaks Hindustani as well as English. Like many Hindu women of her age, she is apparently illiterate and has very little concept of time, being unable to give her own age or the ages of her husband and children. She can, however, give a very comprehensive story of her own life. Her grandfather was Hindi-speaking and came to South Africa from India. Her father was a truck driver on a plantation near Richmond when she was born. He left her mother when the four children were very young, and she had to support them single-handed. Later Mrs Singh's mother left her with her grandmother while she went to Durban to try to find work.

Mrs Singh's husband, who came from New Hanover, was also a driver for a firm in Maritzburg. While Mrs Singh was still living with her grandmother, her future husband's uncle came to ask her grandmother if her granddaughter would marry his nephew. Her granny and aunts were very pleased, but she refused to consent. She says, 'I didn't ever want to get married as I knew I would suffer. But my granny and my auntie begged me to get married. They scolded me and said who's going to look after me when they die? My husband came to see me once before the wedding, but I still didn't want to get married. But the wedding was very nice; it started at ten in the morning and finished at lunch, and then there was lots of nice food. I went to live in New Hanover with my husband and my in-laws, but then after three months it began to get bad. My parents-in-law were very cruel to me. They kept me in the house every day and would not even allow me to go out to the doctor. My husband obeyed his parents and did not care that I suffered. So I took the children and ran away, back to my own mother. My mother blessed me and made me strong. When my in-laws came and took me home, they treated me better as they knew that I might run away again.'

At the temple she talked to many people about their problems, blessed them, and claimed to have healed many in the name of the mother goddess. '*Shakti* is Draupadi, Kali, Lakshmi, Sarasvati – they're all the same. God is one, but takes many forms.' *Shakti* appears to have been the main religious force in Mrs Singh's life and, she claims, has looked after her all her life. *Shakti* never fails to answer her prayers: it was *Shakti* who heard her prayers when her parents-in-law confined her to the house, and later when her husband was 'running around with other women'. '*Shakti* gives strength, peace and food. *Shakti* is the most powerful healer, much more than Shiva or Vishnu, and it is she who gives children. You must pray to her if you want children.' She told of a number of illnesses and misfortunes from which she was delivered by the goddess, as well as stories of how she herself had blessed many women in the name of *Shakti*, after which they produced children. Mrs Singh also comforted people who were dying by blessing them with ash from the temple which, she claimed, helped them to die peacefully.

 184

Mrs Singh insists that the Mother helps all people: women, men and especially children. But she does particularly bestow her enormous power and strength on women. She only gives her power to good women, not to those who do wrong, for example those who harm others, are jealous, show hatred, and don't share with others. Lots of women, she explains, dedicate their lives to *Shakti* and then they do not take husbands or have children. These women often get possessed by *Shakti*. She claims that the *Shakti* trance is the most powerful of all, especially for healing. She herself does not get the trance, and would not like to because 'it's a lot of work'. She maintains that women who get trances often have to neglect their housework and their children because 'lots of people run to trances' in order to be blessed, to solve problems, and to be healed. The trance power, she emphasises, is only used for good purposes, not 'black magic'.

Mrs Singh's mother used to get a very powerful Draupadi trance at the fire-walking festival. She healed many people and carried live coals in her hands without getting burnt. Mrs Singh said she would like to walk across the fire herself, but in Pietermaritzburg the temple committee at that time prohibited women from doing so. However, for many years when she was younger, she was part of the procession that circled the fire every fire-walking day.

Mrs Singh has a shrine in her home where, every morning and evening, she lights the oil lamp and prays before the deities. She explains that before praying it is necessary to bathe and put on clean clothes. A woman should not go into a temple when she is menstruating because, she says, 'This is a dirty thing.' But she immediately qualifies this by adding, 'But Mother made this dirty thing.' Asked about this, she said, 'Shakti doesn't mind if you go near her when you have a period, as long as you bath first and put on all clean things, especially a clean pad.'

Chariots for firewalking

Mrs Naicker, daughter of Mariamman

The extremely fierce-looking elderly woman in a yellow and white sari, her face smeared with yellow turmeric paste indicating that she is possessed by the goddess Mariamman, and holding a clay pot of ashes in her hand, keeps advancing aggressively on groups of people gathered at the goddess festival in Cato Manor in Durban, beckoning them to come forward to get blessed. Every time she lurches forward, people quickly move out of her way in alarm, and then soon crowd round her again. Eventually she appears to be slightly calmer and devotees begin to approach her more confidently, palms pressed together, requesting blessing from this extremely powerful manifestation of the Mother. A number of women hold babies up to be included in the blessing. As the queue of eager people grows longer, each person has a dot of ash from the pot marked on their forehead and Mrs Naiker's turmeric-smeared hand placed heavily on their head. She has gained a reputation as a healer, frequently attracting a queue of people prostrating themselves at her feet. A number of devotees give her money in gratitude for her services.

Mrs Naicker, a widow of over 80 years old who lives in the Indian suburb of Asherville in Durban, has been worshipping the Mother and participating in fire-walking since she was eight years old. She tells how she was born 'a cripple', and her father took a vow that he would walk the fire in order for the Mother to cure

Mrs Naicker, 1993

her, a request that was granted. She soon started walking the fire with him, and has continued to do so every year at the two Durban temples, as well as regularly attending the festival in Pietermaritzburg. Mrs Naicker has become a well-known and much respected figure at goddess festivals, including the annual Gengaiamman festival in Cato Manor, mainly because of her very powerful Mariamman trances. Ordinarily she is a fairly small, demure woman with spectacles and grey hair, tied neatly into a bun. However, when the trance comes upon her, there is a remarkable transformation as she takes off her spectacles, loosens her hair, and smears yellow turmeric paste over her face as an indication of her Mariamman possession. She often carries a clay pot of burning coals and ash on her head. Her demeanour is particularly fierce and commanding so that many people recoil as she lunges towards them grunting, with arms flailing. But they are then drawn to her because of her reputed healing power.

On first being questioned about her trances, some ten years ago, she was very embarrassed and unable to talk about her experiences, apparently because of the socially unacceptable way in which trances cause her to behave. Now, however, she is delighted to greet me at festivals, throwing her arms about me, keen to have her photo taken and to be given copies of these. She appears to 'own' her trances more happily, although she still finds it difficult to talk freely about them. Her attendance at the various goddess festivals is the highlight of her year.

Miss Govinder and the Mother's temple

The elderly Miss Govinder, clad in a sari, welcomes devotees into the small, dark, incense-laden interior of the goddess temple every weekend. About 60 years old, she has full-time employment in a factory in Durban, but serves as the 'priest' in the busy Gengaiamman temple in Cato Manor during the weekends. This temple is a fascinating old wood and iron structure constructed in 1909 over a very large termite mound, which is widely recognised and worshipped as being a manifestation of the great Earth Mother. The mound, which is about two metres high, is 'dressed' in a sari, festooned with garlands and jewellery, and a very popular shrine for offerings and requests for healing.

Miss Govinder's mother served in this temple for most of her life until ill health forced her to retire at the age of 80. She, her daughter emphasises, was totally dedicated to the Mother and also 'had the spirit on her' as she used to get a Mariamman trance which allowed her to heal many people. Miss Govinder was married but has been divorced for many years. She is insistent about being referred to as 'Miss', an indication of her independent status. Years ago she visited India where she spent about a year travelling to many places, about which she recounts numerous stories. In talking of her devotion to the Mother, she emphasises the many healing miracles that she has witnessed during her time at this temple, recounting cures of cancer, helping women to conceive, and assisting in many marital problems. (She lists numerous husbands who are unfaithful, abuse their wives, and misuse alcohol.) The Mother, she says, definitely helps more women than men 'because she's a woman'.

On any visit to this temple it is obvious that it is usually frequented by far more women than men, particularly at the annual festival for the goddess Gangaiamman, the personification of the great Mother Ganges river. This festival, held every Mothers' Day in May, is remarkable in that the men do all the preparation and cooking of the food in large pots over fires in the temple grounds. They then serve the women lunch at long trestle tables, thus treating the women as goddesses for at least this one day in the year.

 190

Mariamman Porridge Festival, 1989

Mrs Jerry's sacrifice for Kali

'You must come to our Kali prayer; we'd love to have you there. It's at our house in Northdale in May.' I met Mrs Jerry Cheddy, usually referred to simply as 'Mrs Jerry', her mother, and her husband Jerry, at the Pietermaritzburg fire-walking festival in 1993. I did not realise that, in accepting their invitation, I would witness one of the world's most primal rituals, reaching back to the roots of human religious experience, one that has survived the centuries and, remarkably, is still performed in the last years of the second millennium, and appears set to continue into the next.

Mrs Jerry's family is from a Hindi background, and the whole family participates regularly in the local annual fire-walking festival. In addition to this, they hold their own private Kali prayer annually at their home to which they invite a large number of friends. Mrs Jerry's mother has been performing this prayer for over 40 years.

On a bright, hot morning the proceedings began down the road, about 100 metres from the house, with the making and blessing of *garagams* – brass pots with a high conical frame decorated with marigold flowers – which represent the goddess, and are carried on devotees' heads. Mrs Jerry and her mother were splendidly dressed, one in a dark red sari, the other wearing yellow, both with garlands of bright orange marigold flowers round their necks. The fierce goddesses – Kali, Mariamman, Draupadi, Gengaiamman and Angalamman – were all then invoked. Mrs Jerry, her mother and husband went into trances,

✿ 192

Mrs Jerry Cheddy, 1992

with the women becoming possessed by Kali, and Jerry possessed by Dee (the north Indian name for Madurai Veeran, one of the male guardians of the fierce goddesses). Both women then had long steel skewers pushed through their tongues, without showing any sense of pain. The women behaved particularly aggressively, letting their hair fall loose, shouting and swirling and dancing with arms outstretched and long hair flailing.

A long procession of devotees, accompanied by much drumming, chanting, and dancing, then made its way up the road to the house where the main participants entered the shrine at the side of the house. All the *garagams* were placed in front of the image of Kali. Mrs Jerry's mother, still in a trance and rocking gently back and forth, stood at the gate to the house and blessed all the visitors who filed past her by placing a dot of ash on their foreheads. Rows of plastic chairs, placed on the grass in front of the shrine, provided seating for visitors. The crowd steadily increased until there were about 120 people at 12.30 p.m., all packed into the very small yard of the house. Bringing the prayer to a climax was the sacrificing of seven male goats and 24 roosters as offerings to Kali, who only accepts male animals. The goats were first marked on their necks with turmeric to purify them, prayers were intoned over them, and all were then very swiftly and cleanly beheaded with a large scythe-like knife to the accompaniment of very loud, frenetic drumming and chanting. Their heads were placed in the shrine before the goddess, and the rest of the carcasses were prepared as a curry to be eaten by the guests as *prasad* (blessed food). All the devotees then shared this sacrificial meal with the goddess, the blood of the sacrifice symbolising a sharing of the same life, thus cementing with her a new bond of peace and friendship. The whole ceremony, from the preparations down the road, through the procession to the final sacrifice, took the form of a colourful, vibrant devotional drama, with Mrs Jerry as the fierce goddess Kali and her husband as the male guardian/companion, ecstatically swirling and dancing round each other.

Walking across fire: Pat Pillay

As the drums beat louder and faster, the woman in a resplendent blood-red sari suddenly began to shake violently. As her body tensed and trembled, her eyes rolled back. Someone loosened her long hair from its neat bun so it tumbled free. She smeared her face with pink *kum-kum* paste, and threw her arms outward, shrieking as the wild goddess possessed her. Then she stood quietly as a long decorated silver skewer was pushed through her tongue, another through her cheeks, and hooks strung with marigolds, limes and coconut shells were pinned through the flesh of her chest and waist. She was now a human manifestation of divinity, and her whole demeanour altered as she became commanding and fierce, emulating the characteristics of the powerful goddess. People began to queue in front of her, some prostrating at her feet, to be blessed by her hand placed on their heads and a dot of ash on their foreheads.

It was Easter Friday in the early nineties and hundreds of worshippers and onlookers had gathered at the Dorpspruit off East Street, at the lower end of Maritzburg, to watch the annual fire-walking festival for the Hindu goddess Draupadi, where this handsome and confident-looking woman was preparing herself to participate in this ancient Tamil ceremony.

Pat (Padmani) Pillay was born in 1958 into a very traditional and conservative Tamil family, in which she says she had an extremely strict upbringing. Her father was a truck driver on the sugar estate at Mount Edgecombe on the KwaZulu-Natal north coast, and her mother caught the train to Durban every day where she worked in a clothing factory. Pat was one of seven sisters and three brothers, none of whom went to school as her parents were too poor to send them.

At this time in the early nineties, Pat lived in Northdale, Pietermaritzburg, with her husband and three children. Their house was very small, with no bathroom or running water, except for a washroom in the back yard. They had no telephone. Both Pat Pillay and her husband had been unemployed for some time. In the small back yard of the house, Pat and her children had constructed a simple wooden shrine to her mother goddess Kali. Made of wood with a tin roof, it had colourful hangings and contained *murtis* and pictures of the goddesses Kali, Durga, Parvati, and other divinities. Pat's whole life and conversation were dominated by her consciousness of the goddess, and by her desire to serve the goddess and the community in every possible way. In fact, she sometimes expressed the wish that she was unencumbered by a family, with no distractions from her full-time service of the goddess, thus showing a typical tension between her *stri-dharma* (womanly duty) to her family, and her *bhakti* or loving devotion to her chosen deity.

Although she has a serious heart problem and suffered a heart attack some years ago, Pat does not take any medication and cannot afford the operation doctors have advised. After the heart attack, she was seriously weak and tired. But, with enormous determination and conscious of the value of her role in the community, she recovered remarkably. She communes with the goddess and 'takes ashes', confident that the Mother will either heal her or 'take' her. In saying this, Pat appears to be completely resigned to the possibility of her own death.

Pat first encountered the worship of the goddess in her grandmother, a Kali devotee, who came to South Africa from south India. She died when Pat was eight years old, but Pat remembers her with great fondness. A year later, Pat experienced her first Kali possession-trance. This did not frighten her as her granny had undergone the same experience, telling Pat that Kali is very caring, even though she is also so powerful. However, Pat's parents were disturbed by this manifestation of the 'spirit', fearing that it would come to dominate her life and prevent her from getting married and having a family.

From this time on, Pat went secretly to the Mariamman temple at Mount Edgecombe, where she continued to worship the goddess. When, after some years, her parents found out about this, they were again very disturbed by her interest. So they encouraged her to marry at the age of fifteen, thinking that this would put an end to her preoccupation with the worship of the Mother. Pat then came to Pietermaritzburg to live with her husband's family.

At eighteen, in 1977, she had her first child, a girl, who apparently had some deformity in her legs. Pat took the child to the Cripple Care Association where she was told that only an operation would help. So Pat went to the temple to ask the Mother Draupadi to help. By this time she was pregnant with her second child, and she said to the Mother, 'The child in me is about to be born, and the child in my hand is a cripple. Have I sinned to deserve this? Please help me.' Then the Mother 'possessed' her and she lost all sense of awareness for a time. When the trance left her, she heard her daughter calling and, as the child walked towards her, Pat realised she was cured. She recognised the Mother's work in this and, since then, regards the Mother as 'the first priority in my life'.

196

Her son, the second child, was born epileptic, and again she appealed to Mother Draupadi. When he was six he made a vow to walk across the fire to honour Draupadi, and has continued to do this for twelve years – he apparently no longer suffers from epilepsy.

During the early eighties, at a sacrifice for the Mother, Pat – possessed by Kali – drank some blood of the sacrificial goats and chickens. Since then she has not menstruated, now regarding herself as 'both a man and a woman for Kali'. Shortly after this Pat started healing and counselling others in her community, for which she has gained a considerable reputation. She insists this comes from Kali: 'Without Mother, I can't do it.' As part of her commitment to the Mother, Pat never cuts her hair. Shortly after this appearance of Kali, her 'marriage relationship became very unsuccessful' and she had to tell her husband that she no longer wanted sexual relations with him.

To do most of this work, Pat goes to her temple and calls on the Mother to hear her, being answered by a powerful Kali trance in which she believes she actually

Pat Pillay with skewers and hooks in her flesh
at the Draupadi Firewalking Festival

becomes Kali, acting and speaking as the goddess. Her healing work covers a range of ailments and community problems, such as curing sterility in women; helping women who are experiencing problems with husbands who are unfaithful, drink too much, beat them, or abandon them; helping young girls to find husbands; and exorcising evil spirits from houses. She tells a number of stories to illustrate her success in helping women who have been told by doctors that they are unable to have children, and how she has invoked the help of Mother Kali. These women are then assured that if they go home, trusting the power of the Mother, they will fall pregnant. In a number of instances, this is what has happened. With heart problems, she 'does a prayer' to the Mother and then gives the person ash, which he or she can mix with sugar water and drink, or rub on the body and forehead. Pat has also been consulted by people with skin problems, which she treats by telling them to put ash and cow's urine in their baths. (Because of the Mother's nurturing capacity, the cow

 198

is regarded as a manifestation of her, so all five products of the cow – milk, *ghee*, curds, urine and dung – are considered to be particularly holy and curative.) Husbands who drink too much and cause trouble at home are severely dealt with by the Mother (Pat speaking in a trance), and told they must give up the drink. On many occasions they apparently improve dramatically because of the Mother's censure. Even if the husbands will not come to see her, Pat says the wives are helped as the *darshan* of being in the presence of the Mother 'gives them marvellous support'.

Because news of these successes has spread, Pat now has so many people wanting to consult her that she has since the early nineties set aside three evenings a week to deal with this demand. Each evening, from twenty-five to forty people – Hindus, Muslims and some Christians – arrive to seek healing, advice or simply the *darshan* of the goddess in Pat. Then Pat, sitting cross-legged on the floor of the shrine, rocking gently back and forth in her trance, speaks as the powerful goddess Kali, and the people, either singly or in family groups, tell her their problems. These consultations usually last late into the evening. People 'pay' for Pat's services, either by leaving a gift of money or, at a later stage – if a favourable result has been obtained, by giving her things such as *puja* items (*agarbhati*, pictures of deities, etc.), jewellery, or saris.

When she wishes to call Kali to participate in the evening sessions at her home, she goes into her shrine, stands before the *murti* of Kali, lights incense and camphor on a tray, and calls the Mother. Then she 'feels her coming closer'. She smells the incense as overpowering, filling her with the 'most beautiful smell in the world. And then she comes, and the mountain falls on my shoulders!' She then claims she remembers nothing until she comes out of the trance, perhaps an hour or more later. But she knows that during this time she is Kali, and Kali speaks through her mouth. Somehow she has been unconscious on the ordinary level of awareness and operating at some deeper level, although she obviously retains some sense of what is happening, showing recognition of people and awareness of the location of various objects. She is very interested in photographs of herself taken while she is in a trance, and is sometimes surprised at how she looks and behaves. After the trance she says she feels 'like I ran very far; I've gone a long distance, I'm tired and my knees are paining, so that I need to sit down. But I am very happy, and feel very good. I usually drink some milk or sugar water which helps give me back the energy which she has used.'

Pat also performs prayers in which she helps 'the spirit to come out' in other women, so that they too may experience the goddess-possessing power in their lives. With Pat's encouragement, her sister Tillie (Yogavallie) Moonsamy has recently experienced possession trances, and has walked across the fire in Durban. Increasingly Pat is invited to attend privately organised goddess ceremonies where she is believed to bring with her, and to manifest, the presence of Kali. Her presence is regarded as adding sanctity to the rituals.

Pat's devotion to the goddess has resulted in her participation in the Draupadi fire-walking festival, and through this was brought into a protracted clash with the Pietermaritzburg temple committee of the Mariamman temple, where the ceremony is held. For many years, longer than anyone could remember, the all-male committee only permitted men to walk across the fire, whereas at the two Durban temples both women and men were allowed to walk. Women in Pietermaritzburg were able to participate in all the preparatory activities leading up to the fire-walking climax of the festival, even to being a very obvious presence in the final procession to the temple. But, on arrival at the firepit, only the men were allowed to cross the fire while the women were confined to circumambulating the pit and encouraging the men.

This discrimination caused considerable distress to numbers of women over recent years but, generally, they accepted the situation as being beyond their control: if this was the decision of the men of the temple committee, there must be good reasons for it. It was not for them to criticise – certainly not publicly.

Pat and a number of other women who earnestly wished to participate in a fire-walk, and who had the necessary transport, travelled to one or both of the Durban temples every year. Here they were welcomed and encouraged to participate in the entire festival. In Durban, Pat was finally able to fulfil her wish to undertake this greatest of all austerities for the Mother. Together with other women, Pat was able to come through the fire unscathed year after year, an achievement which brings a considerable sense of empowerment.

 200

Because of the Pietermaritzburg temple committee's ban on women walking, Pat was unable to accompany her son in his fire-walking at that temple. Since about 1990 when her eldest daughter was only thirteen years old, both Pat's daughters have also walked the fire in Durban and are excited to be part of this tradition. Pat's elder daughter recently experienced her first trance and, like her mother, welcomes being possessed by the goddess. At each fire-walking festival, Pat – resplendent in a red sari (Kali's colour) and accompanied by her three children – has become a familiar and respected figure. When, during the period of preparation immediately before the walk, she hears the drums beginning to beat and smells the incense, she goes into a trance and remains in this state until after she has walked through the fire, a period of about one to one-and-a-half hours. As she goes into the trance, she loosens her hair and smears her face with pink *kum-kum* paste, a sign that it is Kali who possesses her – rather like putting on the mask of the goddess. Her whole mild demeanour changes as she assumes the character of the fierce, uncontrollable Kali. Her muscles tense, her eyes grow large and staring, and she often grunts and cries out loudly in a somewhat alarming fashion. She becomes an extremely commanding and fierce woman as she gestures for one of her chosen devotees to push long skewers through her tongue and cheeks. The hooks pierced through the skin of her chest have strings of marigolds, limes and coconut shells. Because the skewers through her tongue prevent her from speaking, she grunts and gestures to people to approach and be blessed with ash from her tray of burning camphor, which she places on their foreheads. Many people prostrate themselves at her feet as she is now the divinity Kali herself.

Explaining why she participates in the fire-walk, Pat says: 'This is the Mother's day, once a year. We need to feed her; it's our yearly offering to her and we sacrifice our all to her. We need to ask her forgiveness and lay our burdens on her. She will cleanse us and renew us. It's a new start, like new year, and she will carry us through the year. Walking on the fire is proving your *sati* [purity] to people. You carry Mother Draupadi on your shoulder over the pit, and you are saying to her, "I can carry you and take your responsibility; I am totally dedicated to you."'

When she is in a trance, Pat neither feels the skewers and hooks in her flesh, nor the heat of the fire when she walks across it, although she wishes she could. Often she also places a burning block of camphor on her tongue. Explaining why she does these austerities, she says, 'I am sacrificing my all, my flesh, my body, myself, everything, to her.'

While looking at photographs of herself and other people in trances, she suddenly put her hand to her face and said, 'I feel that the Mother is calling me; my head gets heavy; I feel strange, but I don't want to go now.' (Pat has learnt to control her trances and can enter and exit at will.)

Talking about what the Mother means to her, she says, 'She is everywhere; look outside, she is there. She is the silent listener. She comes to me in my sleep; in a deep sleep she comes, and she comforts me, she cheers me up. She says to me, "There is no suffering for you; you will not suffer." I would sacrifice everything for her. I depend on her for everything; she meets my needs, my dreams, my all. I don't want money, I don't want diamonds or a big house. My dream is to have a beautiful temple for the Mother; that's my dream home for her. Yes, I feel she uses more women than men; she will be more secure with them because women's bodies are closer to her than men's. She uses your body, your *bottu* [red dot on

201

the forehead], your *thali* [wedding thread worn round the neck], and your *manja* [turmeric colour on the face]. Yes, she has all that. When it comes to young women's bodies, she purifies them and makes them clean.'

In 1996, Pat felt the time had come to make some public protest about the exclusion of women from the Pietermaritzburg fire-walk. She felt increasingly unhappy about this blatant discrimination against women who form part of the core of worshippers at this temple. The reasons that the all-male temple committee gave for banning women were that women might trip on their saris

Pat Pillay walking the fire

and fall into the fire, which apparently did happen many years ago; and, probably more importantly, that women are rendered ritually unclean by menstruation and should not participate in worship during that time. Pat, however, was unhappy with both reasons. She pointed out that men who wear long *dhotis* might just as easily trip, and that in Cato Manor a woman did trip and fall, but that no-one considered this a reason to forbid all women from walking. With regard to the issue of menstruation, she explained that in general women are credited with knowing when and when not to participate in public worship, and no-one else should attempt to decide this for them. (She also pointed out that she and other post-menopausal women are excluded from this concern, anyway). All devotees, she said, are highly aware of the necessity to be humble and pure when they come before deities, and only the Mother can see into people's hearts and minds where true purity lies.

What gave her most pain, however, was the unfairness of this ban. 'If other temples can welcome us and allow us to walk, why not here? The committee can't choose who will walk and who can't. Everything is decided among the men, and the women are just left out. Women are being stopped from carrying out their calling to worship the Mother. Woman is Draupadi; she is closer to the Mother than men because she has the same body as Mother. Women can pin, get the trance, bless, join in the procession, but when the time comes to walk, they are told, "You are dirt." And this is a woman's festival!' And in a remarkable flash of feminist insight, she continued: 'I think the men are threatened by us because we are closer to the Mother than they are; the men are frightened of our power. They want to have more power than the women, so they won't treat us as their equals.'

So Pat arranged an interview with *The Natal Witness*, the local daily newspaper, and an article expressing her concern was published on Monday 15 April 1996, with a photo of Pat, a week after the local fire-walking festival. When asked how she would respond if the temple committee reacted negatively to her views, she said, 'Let the sky blow! I hope they come to me; I'll talk to them. Am I wrong or am I right?'

There was much positive response from the public. The newspaper offices had about 25 phone calls, mainly from women who wished to consult Pat about various

203

ailments, and a few to support her call for the inclusion of women in fire-walking. Pat reported that the number of people attending her evening sessions rose quite considerably, including a couple of White women who came requesting healing. She reckoned about 46 women assured her that, given the opportunity, they would walk across the fire.

Most encouraged by this response, Pat was determined to follow her challenge through until the temple committee responded. She said, 'I don't need to fight for myself. I can walk in Durban, but some women haven't got the vehicles to get there. They need to walk here. I am fighting for them. I am very angry; from now till the day I die I will go at the committee till they change. I feel really super about all the women who have contacted me. Until the committee says, "Okay, at least give women a chance," I will not rest.'

The elderly temple *pujari* was adamant that women should not be allowed to walk as 'they get very fierce trances and could get burnt by falling into the fire'. He claimed that no women had ever indicated to the men that they wished to walk, and dismissed Pat's article as 'just for publicity'. Using a traditional patriarchal argument advanced by men who claim to know what is best for women, he assured me that the temple committee had the women's best interests at heart in not allowing them to walk. The young Sri Lankan *Kurukkal* priest, however, conceded that the situation would need to be looked into. He admitted he was aware that women participate in fire-walking in India, and that this could carry weight in deciding the local conflict. The priest agreed that it was probably only a matter of time before there would be change as the reasons were not good enough to continue resisting the women's request.

Two weeks after the initial newspaper article, *The Sunday Times* – the largest national weekly paper – interviewed Pat and published an article entitled 'Temple takes heat over ban on women'. The chairperson of the temple committee, asked to give reasons for their ban on women, claimed that the decision was taken 'after some women tripped over their saris and fell into the glowing embers ... Some of the women also suffered nasty burns on their feet. Women have tender feet and burn easily.' He added that 'another reason for keeping women away was to control

 204

the number of people participating in the fire-walking ceremony ... as our temple ... has a small area where the fire-walking takes place ...' But he denied that his committee was sexist or discriminated against women. However, he conceded, 'If any of them make representations to us to lift the ban, we will certainly discuss this at our meeting.'

With the help of friends, Pat then drafted a short petition calling on the temple committee to lift their ban on women, which was signed by 89 people. This she presented at the temple office a few days before the annual general meeting. But, although the matter was raised at the meeting, no decision was taken. It became clear that the men would not easily be persuaded to change. Indeed, they seemed to be very threatened by the women, and the chairperson dismissed Pat as a 'troublemaker who runs a backyard temple cult'.

A year later, in 1997, at the Pietermaritzburg fire-walking, Pat decided that she would walk across the fire, despite all prohibitions. As the long procession of devotees approached the temple, Pat in a Kali trance, her sister Tillie, and a number of male supporters attempted to enter the crowd-control barriers that led the participants to the edge of the firepit. In spite of all efforts to prevent her, she and Tillie managed to push their way through and jumped onto the coals from the side of the pit just as a loud rumble of thunder rolled across the darkening sky. As her feet touched the coals, Pat began to dance, the coconuts pinned to her chest flying from side to side. The crowd at the edge of the pit roared its encouragement as she and Tillie made their way halfway across the pit. Then a large official leapt into the pit and lifted her out. Tillie was pushed out more roughly as pandemonium broke out, with some yelling their approval and others calling to 'close' the pit to prevent other devotees from coming across. These men appeared to consider that the women's presence on the coals had contaminated the pit. However, other participants continued to run across and the rest of the procession of male fire-walkers crossed without further interruption or mishap. Pat says she began to realise what had happened when she found herself surrounded by well-wishers, many of them throwing their arms round her. All around her people were saying, 'The women walked!' 'Pat, you did it!' And Pat's first question, because she had been in a trance and did not remember what had happened, was, 'Did she dance, did the Mother dance?' Many women wept because they wished they had walked, and some said, 'We have waited a long time for this.' And the general feeling among the women was that the thunder and lightning was the Mother expressing her anger at the ban on women, and her approval of what had been accomplished in her name. Of course, those against the women maintained that the thunder was the Mother indicating her disapproval.

Commenting on this development in her work for the Mother, Pat said, 'I had decided that I had to break the rules. Somebody had to do something to make them agree to their wrong, and let us walk. We need communication and friendship between the women and the men, not a barrier. Mother Shakti created two sexes – the men must do their task and the women must do theirs. They must both serve her at the temple. I am not educated but, when it comes to Mother Shakti, I have knowledge, wisdom and power. And still they refuse to hear me. I have to fight for her, and fight for the women. Mother is making me a totally different person. She makes me happy every day. She gives me strength to go on. She supplies my daily needs. She's always there for me.'

 206

The following year, 1998, the fire-walk attracted a considerable amount of bad press for the temple, precipitated by the temple committee's last minute call for a fee of R20 from all those who wished to cross the fire. Considerable dissatisfaction was expressed and the committee made no statement on whether or not women would be allowed to participate, even when they were pressed by a *Natal Witness* reporter the day before the event. A number of people then had to be hospitalised after being burnt as they crossed the fire. Again, the chairperson of the temple committee responded somewhat aggressively to criticism in the press, threatening legal action against those who voiced disapproval of his decisions. Most significantly, he stated: 'We have excluded women from walking across the fire in the past. We realise that we are the only temple which practises this discrimination and this year we did call for women to walk across the fire, but none came forward. We will meet with the women a few weeks ahead of the next fire-walking and discuss with them how we will accommodate them.' Pat said that as far as she and the other women were aware, there was no such call. Pat said that someone who was at the firepit after everyone had walked told her an official then announced, 'Where are the women; aren't they going to walk?' but that no women present were prepared to come forward at that late stage. However, this statement from the committee was important and Pat was determined that the next year women would at last participate fully in the festival.

And this, finally, is what happened. The temple committee capitulated to popular pressure and bad publicity. It announced, when approached by a reporter from *The Natal Witness* two days before the ceremony, that the ban against women had been lifted. So, on Friday 2 April 1999, several women successfully crossed the fire, amid much rejoicing from their supporters. Tillie, quoted in the news on the following Monday, said, 'It wasn't me, it was Ma Kali doing the walking.'

Seven years on, women have become an accepted and highly visible part of the procession and the fire-walk. The indignities and injustices they suffered from the ban on their full participation are a thing of the past.

Many people still come to sit in Pat's small shrine and listen to her talking compellingly and charismatically about the Mother. 'And I talk and talk, and they listen. They feel good; it's a *darshan*, an education.'

Glossary

agarbhati: incense

ahimsa: 'non-harmfulness'; abstaining from causing injury to any living being

Amman: 'mother', 'respected woman'; used as part of the name of many indigenous south Indian goddesses

ananda: 'bliss', 'joy'; added to the end of a male renunciate's name in the Ramakrishna Movement

Angalamman: an indigenous south Indian Amman goddess

arati: see *arti*

arguwa: a person who negotiates marriage connections

arsh: the throne of God

arti: the ritual of waving a lamp in front of a deity

Aryans: the name of the Sanskrit-speaking Indo-European peoples who migrated into India from 1500 BCE; they referred to themselves as 'arya' (pure) to distinguish themselves from the aboriginal inhabitants of the country

Arya Samaj: a reformed Hindu group formed in India in 1875 by Dayanand Saraswati, which was introduced into South Africa in 1905

asanas: yogic postures

ashram: a religious institution for retreat and meditation

ashramas: the four traditional stages of life through which a Hindu male is traditionally expected to progress: *Brahmacharya*, the stage of the unmarried student of religion; *Grihastha*, the householder stage; *Vanaprastha*, the forest-dweller or hermit stage; *Sannyasa*, the renunciate or ascetic stage

atman: the eternal soul or spirit, the essential self; this experiences a succession of mortal lives until *moksha* brings release

Aum (Om): the original sacred sound or mantra; the most sacred and profound name and symbol of divinity; it is chanted at the commencement of prayers and religious ceremonies, and in meditation

avatar/avatara: incarnation, usually of the God Vishnu, for example Krishna and Rama

babouches: slippers

Bhagavad Gita: possibly the most popular of the Hindu scriptures, it is a small part of the great epic, the *Mahabharata*; it is sometimes simply called the *Gita*

bhaiya: brother

bhajans: religious songs used in congregational worship

bhakti: loving devotion to God

Bhojpuri: a dialect of Hindi spoken by people from the Bhojpur district of the Madhya Pradesh state of India

bottu: red dot of *kum-kum* on the forehead

bowla: a vessel containing glowing coals

Brahmacharya: the first *ashrama* of life – the stage of the celibate student of the scriptures (*Brahmchari*)

Brahman: the Absolute or Ultimate Reality – changeless, formless, indescribable, all-pervading

Brahmanical: having continuity with the ancient scriptural traditions: the *Vedas* and *Upanishads*

Brahmans (Brahmins): the highest of the four *varnas*; priests – uphold and teach the ancient Brahmanical traditions

caay/chai: tea, usually boiled with the milk and sugar already added

chapatti: flat, unleavened wholemeal Indian bread

choombu: a small brass pot

dalit: 'oppressed'; the preferred name for the Untouchables or outcastes – those who do not have a place in the caste system

darshan: receiving good spiritual vibrations by being in the presence of divinity, either in the form of an actual deity or some other manifestation of divinity such as a guru or possessed person

Deepavali: see *Diwali*

Devi/Maha Devi: one of the generic names for the great goddess

Devi Mahatmya: 'glory of the Divine Mother'; the Sanskrit text of 700 verses which celebrates the victory of the great Mother (Maha Devi) over various demons or enemies of the gods; it is part of the *Markandeya Purana* which, among other accounts, contains the story of Durga slaying the Buffalo Demon; it is regularly chanted as part of the worship of Kali and Durga

dhal/dholl: a term for members of the pulse and legume family, as well as for the sauce made from these which is used as an accompaniment to other dishes

dharma: law; sacred and social duty; custom; religion; cosmic order

dholl: see *dhal*

dhoti: a loincloth worn by men consisting of a single piece of cloth wound round the waist

diaspora: literally 'dispersion'; used of the worldwide Indian communities in countries other than the Indian homeland

didi: sister

Divali: see *Diwali*

Diwali/Divali/Deepavali: one of the most popular Hindu festivals in which the homecoming of the deities Rama and Sita, after their exile, is celebrated; a festival of light where rows of small lamps are placed in gardens and temples, fireworks are used, and gifts are exchanged

Draupadi: the heroine of the great epic, the *Mahabharata*; the goddess of fire-walking

Dravidians: probably the original inhabitants of India, they are predominant in the east and south of the country; Tamil and Telugu are the Dravidian languages represented in South Africa

Durga: the great goddess in her form as demon-slayer; the name means 'invincible'

epics: the *Mahabharata* and *Ramayana*, both north Indian works dating from 200 BCE – 200 CE; Krishna is the main deity (*avatar*) of the former and Rama of the latter

Ganga/Gengaiamman: the water goddess; as Ganga, she is a Brahmanical goddess of the River Ganges, but this is also the name of one of the south Indian Amman goddesses

garagam/karagam/goron gon: a decorated pot, used in Amman goddess festivals; believed to be a manifestation of the goddess

Gengaiamman: see *Ganga*

ghee: clarified butter; used as an offering, particularly in the *havan* ceremony; also used in cooking

Gita: abbreviated form of the *Bhagavad Gita*

goron gon: see *garagam*

 212

Grihastha: the householder *ashrama*; the second stage of life

Gujarati/Gujerati: the language of the state of Gujarat in north India; an Indo-Aryan language; one of the four Hindu language groups in South Africa

Gujerati: see *Gujarati*

gulli-danda: a game of tip cat played with a short stick

guru/guruji: a teacher of religious knowledge; a spiritual guide or teacher

guruji: see *guru*

Gurukkal: see *Kurukkal*

hajj: the pilgrimage to Mecca that every Muslim should make once in a lifetime

halaal: food prepared according to Muslim dietary requirements

haldee: see *hardee*

Hanuman: the monkey God, a faithful devotee of Rama

hardee: yellow powder from the root of the turmeric plant

havan/homa: a fire offering to a deity of substances such as ghee, petals, and *samagree* (a mixture of aromatic dried bark, flowers, etc.); a modification of the ancient Vedic fire sacrifice particularly advocated by the Arya Samaj

Hindi: an Indo-Aryan language; one of the four Hindu language groups in South Africa

Holi: a Hindu festival celebrating the defeat of Holika, a demon, often with the burning of an effigy and much boisterous rejoicing; the youthful Lord Krishna is also honoured at this time; in the northern hemisphere it marks the advent of spring

homa: see *havan*

Indra: the Vedic god of thunder and rain

Indra pooja: the prayer for the rain god Indra

ISKCON: International Society for Krishna Consciousness (Hare Krishna)

jhanda: a red, triangular-shaped flag usually flown from a bamboo pole, erected as part of a Hindu ceremony in honour of the deity Hanuman

jihad: literally 'effort', 'striving'; Muslim holy war; sometimes used to denote a crusade in support of a cause

Kali: the great goddess in her fiercest manifestation; 'Mother Time'

kanya-daan: the giving away of the bride by her parents which, traditionally, implies that the bride is handed over from her father's care and responsibility to that of her husband

karagam: see *garagam*

karma: 'actions' or 'deeds'; the spiritual law controlling rebirth (*samsara*), which states that a person's actions will be rewarded or punished in future reincarnations or states of existence

Kavadi: a Tamil festival devoted to the god Soobramoniar/Muruga

Krishna: an *avatar* (incarnation) of the great god Vishnu whose consort is Radha

Kshatriyas: the second of the *varnas* – traditionally warriors and rulers

kulu: sour porridge

kum-kum: vermilion; the pink powder made from the red berries of the kamala tree, used for the *bottu* (*tilak*) dot on the forehead; a symbol of fertility used by married women; also used in *puja* (prayer or worship) and at festivals

Kurukkal/Gurukkal: a south Indian school of Brahman priests

kutirs: Sanskrit for 'house' or 'residence'

Lakshmi: the goddess consort of Vishnu; goddess of good fortune

Laws of Manu: a well-known law book, probably from the second or third century BCE, attributed to the sage Manu

lingam: the phallus; the sacred pillar; the main symbol of Shiva's powers of fertility, and the most popular focus for his worship

lota: a brass, vase-like container used in religious ceremonies

madrassa: a school attached to a mosque, usually to teach Arabic and the study of the *Quran*

Maha: 'great', for example Mahabharata ('great war of the Bharatas') and Mahatma ('great soul')

Mahabharata: the 'great war of the Bharatas'; one of the two great epics of Hinduism whose theme is the war between the Kauravas and the Pandavas

Maha Devi: see *Devi*

Mahisasura: the Buffalo Demon destroyed by Durga; the story is contained in the *Devi Mahatmya*

 214

mala: a beaded necklace

mama: an uncle

mandir: a temple, usually of reformed Hinduism; in South Africa, Arya Samaj places of worship are referred to as *mandirs*

manja: turmeric colour on the face

mantra: a sacred word or phrase (e.g. Aum/Om) used to assist in concentration or meditation; often given to a pupil by a guru; sometimes used as a synonym for 'prayer'

Mariamman: one of the indigenous south Indian goddesses believed to be the cause and cure of pox diseases

Mata: 'mother'; another name for the Mother goddess

mihrab: a niche in a mosque indicating the direction of Mecca

moksha: the final liberation or release from the cycle of rebirth (*samsara*)

mosque: a Muslim place of worship, usually with a minaret

Moulvi: a Muslim teacher

Mughal: the Muslim dynasty of Indian emperors established in 1526; under the emperor Akbar (1556–1605), there was a golden age of arts and literature

mundap: the canopy raised for ceremonial purposes

murti: the visible image of a deity

Om: see *Aum*

pacha pandal/pundal: literally 'green tent/canopy'; a canopy built with greenery and erected for wedding ceremonies

Parvati: 'daughter of the mountain'; goddess consort of Shiva

pooja: see *puja*

Poongavana Amman: one of the indigenous south Indian goddesses

porridge prayer: a prayer held for the fierce goddesses (e.g. Mariamman and Draupadi); it involves the offering of sour porridge (*kulu*) and other 'cooling' foods such as milk, coconut and pumpkin, in order to cool the anger of the goddess as well as the fever she may have inflicted on her victims; the porridge is also eaten by devotees during the festival

prasad: a holy or blessed substance such as food, ash or incense that has been offered to a deity; *prasad* is believed to be physically and spiritually beneficial to those who receive it

puja/pooja: prayer; worship of a deity or its image, or of a person regarded as representing a deity

pujari: one who assists at *puja*; a temple assistant; in South Africa, an assistant to the priest

pundal: see *pacha pandal*

pundit/pandit: a Hindu religious teacher; *punditha* is the female form

punditji: priest

Puranas: Hindu scriptures containing much popular mythological and devotional material

purdah: the custom of screening women from men; women wearing clothing that conceals them when they go out of the house

Quran/Koran: the Muslim scriptures

raagi: a kind of vegetable

Radha: goddess lover of Krishna

rajamah: kingly or royalty

Rama: the hero of the great epic, the *Ramayana*; an *avatar* (incarnation) of the god Vishnu; husband of Sita

Ramakrishna Mission/Movement: a reformed Hindu group formed in 1887 by Vivekanada, a disciple of the mystic Ramakrishna; the Ramakrishna Centre of South Africa was founded in 1946

Ramayana: 'The Adventures of Rama', one of the two great epics of Hinduism

sabha: society, as in Maha Sabha

sadhana: spiritual practices

Sai Baba: born in south India in 1926, believed to be an incarnation of divinity, and attracting huge numbers of followers, with many Sathya Sai Baba groups in South Africa

samagree: a mixture of dried bark (e.g. sandlewood), flowers and spices, which give off an aromatic fragrance when burnt; used in religious offerings such as *havan*

 216

samsara: the cycle of birth, death, rebirth that all people experience

samskara: life-cycle rituals, such as naming a child, marriage, funeral rites

sandhya: the morning and evening lighting of a lamp and prayers at the shrine of the family deities, often performed by the mother of the house

Sannyasa: the fourth of the *ashramas* – the renunciate or ascetic stage

sannyasi: one who has renounced all earthly attachments; an ascetic, living in the fourth of the *ashramas*, the stage of *Sannyasa*; *sanyasini* is the female form

Sanskrit: Indo-European language of the Aryans; the sacred language of Hindu scriptures

Saptapadi: Seven Steps, each step representing a promise by new marriage partners for each other's welfare, support, prosperity, long life, and so on

Sarasvati: goddess consort of Brahma; goddess of knowledge and learning

Sati: 'the good or pure woman'; the earliest name for the consort of Shiva who burnt herself to death in the sacrificial fire, thus giving her name to the practice of the self-immolation of widows

satsang (satsangh): 'sat' means 'truth' and 'sang' means 'association'; the regular congregational worship of reformed Hindu groups incorporating prayers, songs, and readings from scriptures; communal worship

satyagraha: non-violent action, a term coined by Gandhi during his stay in South Africa

seva: service

Shaivite: a follower of the god Shiva

Shakta: a follower of Shakti, the goddess

Shakti: the 'power' and 'energy' of the goddess; a generic name for the goddess

Shiva: one of the great deities of Hinduism

Shivarathri: 'the night of Shiva'; an annual festival honouring Lord Shiva

shri/sri: an honorific for important people

sirdar: in the colonial context, an Indian leader or overseer of a group of indentured labourers

Sita: goddess; wife of Rama; heroine of the *Ramayana*; often presented to Hindu women as the model of the ideal wife

souks: small shops in an Arab market or bazaar

sri: see *shri*

stri-dharma: womanly duty

sudras: the fourth and lowest of the *varnas* – labourers

swami: a respected religious figure or spiritual guide; usually an initiate of a religious order

tajines: the earthenware dishes with conical lids used for preparing Moroccan spicy stew, also known as 'tajine'

Tamil: a south Indian Dravidian language; one of the four language groups of Hindus in South Africa

tapas: 'heat'; the great spiritual power that is gained by practising austerities and ascetic disciplines

Telugu: a south Indian Dravidian language; one of the four language groups of Hindus in South Africa

thali: yellow wedding thread worn round the neck

tilak (bottu): the dot applied to the forehead as a blessing, usually made with *kum-kum*, ash, or sandal paste, which marks the spot of the 'third eye' representing spiritual insight; also the dot placed on the forehead of married women as a mark of their fertility

trisula: the trident, which usually belongs to Shiva, but also to the fierce goddesses

turmeric: yellow powder from the root of the turmeric plant (also known as *haldee/hardee*); saffron was traditionally the colour of royalty and turmeric is a cheaper substitute; it is regarded as purifying, cooling and healing, and is much used in religious contexts, for example to bless devotees, to cool/heal a person with fever, and to bathe images of deities as well as brides

ummrah: a lesser *hajj*

***Upanishads*:** early Hindu scriptures, appended to the *Vedas*

Vaishnavites: followers of Vishnu

vaishyas: the third of the *varnas* – merchant or business class

Vanaprastha: the *ashrama* of the forest dweller, the third stage of life, which has become virtually obsolete

 218

varna(s): 'colour'; the four main classes into which Hindu society is hierarchically divided

Vedanta: 'end of the *Vedas*'; a Hindu philosophical school; being in continuity with the Upanishadic tradition; *Neo-Vedanta* is the term used for a branch of the reformed tradition, stemming largely from Ramakrishna and maintaining the essential divinity of all humans

***Vedas*:** the oldest Hindu scriptures, probably composed between 1500–1000 BCE, and reflecting Aryan beliefs

vibhuti: holy ash; Hindus regard ash as the purest substance because it is all that remains when matter is burnt; ash can also remind one of the impermanence of matter; *vibhuti* is used to bless and to cure a variety of ailments – being placed on the forehead, rubbed on the body, or eaten

Vishnu: one of the great deities of Hinduism

vrata: a personal vow to a deity, often involving austerities such as fasting, *pujas*, pilgrimages, and rituals such as fire-walking

yajna: sacrifice; the central act of Vedic religion; in the neo-Hindu Arya Samaj movement, animal sacrifice has been completely abandoned and replaced by offerings of fruit, flowers, and incense

yoni: female genitals, the counterpart of the *lingam* (phallus); sometimes refers to the procreative agent of the universe, the 'Universal Womb' (Stutley, 1985:125)

zakaah: the Muslim charitable giving of two and a half per cent of one's excess wealth or income; that which is left after all living expenses have been catered for

References

Beall, J. 1990. Women under indentured labour in colonial Natal. In Walker, C. (Ed.) *Women and Gender in Southern Africa to 1945*. Cape Town: David Philip: 146–167.

Bhana, S. and Pachai, B. (Eds.) 1984. *A Documentary History of Indian South Africans*. Cape Town: David Philip.

Diesel, A. 1998a. The empowering image of the Divine Mother: A South African woman worshipping the goddess. In *Journal of Contemporary Religion*, 13(1): 73–90.

Diesel, A. 1998b. The veneration of the goddess as an empowering symbol for both Hindu and contemporary feminist women: with special reference to the worship of the Hindu Amman goddesses in KwaZulu-Natal. Unpublished PhD thesis. Pietermaritzburg: University of Natal.

Diesel, A. 2002. Tales of women's suffering: Draupadi and other Amman goddesses as role models for women. In *Journal of Contemporary Religion*, 17(1): 5–20.

Diesel, A. and Maxwell, P. 1993. *Hinduism in Natal: A Brief Introduction*. Pietermaritzburg: University of Natal Press.

Freund, B. 1995. *Insiders and Outsiders: The Indian Working Class of Durban 1910–1990.* Pietermaritzburg: University of Natal Press.

Kuper, H. 1960. *Indian People in Natal.* Pietermaritzburg: University of Natal Press.

Lemon, A. 1990. The political position of Indians in South Africa. In Clarke, C., Peach, C. and Vertovec, S. (Eds.) *South Asians Overseas: Migration and Ethnicity.* Cambridge: Cambridge University Press: 131–148.

Pillay, G.J., Naidoo, T. and Dangor, S. 1989. Religious profile. In Arkin, A.J., Magyar, K.P. and Pillay, G.J. (Eds.) *The Indian South Africans.* Pinetown: Owen Burgess: 143–170.

Stutley, M. 1985. *Hinduism: The Eternal Law.* Wellingborough, Northhamptonshire: The Aquarian Press.

The Victoria & Albert Museum. n.d. *Shamiana: The Mughal Tent.* Two brochures.

Wills, T. 1988. The segregated city. In Laband, J. and Haswell, R. (Eds.) *Pietermaritzburg: A New Portrait of an African City.* Pietermaritzburg: University of Natal Press and Shuter & Shooter.

221